Books by Dave Meurer

Boyhood Daze
Daze of Our Wives

DAZE of Our WiVeS

A SEMI-HELPFUL Guide to Marital Bliss

DAVE MEURER

BETHANY HOUSE PUBLISHERS
MINNEAPOLIS, MINNESOTA 55438

Cover illustration by Paula Becker
Cover design by Lookout Design Group, Inc.

Published by Bethany House Publishers
A Ministry of Bethany Fellowship International
11400 Hampshire Avenue South
Minneapolis, Minnesota 55438
www.bethanyhouse.com

Printed in the United States of America by
Bethany Press International, Minneapolis, Minnesota 55438

Library of Congress Cataloging-in-Publication Data

Meurer, Dave, 1958–
   Daze of our wives : a semi-helpful guide to marital bliss / by
Dave Meurer.
      p. cm.
   ISBN 0–7642–2342–9 (pbk.)
    1. Marriage—Humor. 2. Marriage—Religious aspects.
I. Title.
HQ518.M475   2000   99–051017
306.81—dc21   CIP

For Dale,
my wife,
the love of my life.

DAVE MEURER works for the United States House of Representatives as a field representative for a California congressman. He is the winner of numerous state and national writing awards and honors. His writings have appeared in major publications, including *Focus on the Family* and *Homelife*. The Meurer family lives in northern California.

Dave Meurer can be reached at Meurerdaze@aol.com or by writing to Bethany House Publishers, 11400 Hampshire Ave. So., Minneapolis, MN 55438.

Acknowledgments

Behind every successful male humor writer who decides to pen a marriage book stands a woman with nervous, darting eyes who keeps saying, "You aren't *seriously* planning on putting *that* in the book, are you?"

And when the humor writer says, "Sure!" she will get these really taut muscles in her neck and you can literally watch her transform into one of those grim and humorless people who used to work as an official censor in the old Soviet Union.

The mortified expression "You can't put *that* in" is most often related to something about sex, such as this passage in chapter 5:

"Now, what kind of God would create intelligent and rational creatures, loftily made in the very image of himself, and then imbue them with a powerful impulse that can rapidly turn them into the mental equivalent of scrap iron? The answer is, obviously, the kind of God who wants many more of us! And if you will look at population demographics, His plan is certainly working!"

So first and foremost in my list of acknowledgments, I would like to acknowledge that my wife, Dale, did not physically harm me during the course of my penning this book. This was quite an accomplishment on her part (although she did exclaim *"Nyet!"* quite a bit and also took to wearing sturdy Russian boots).

Actually, she was an amazingly good sport and extremely supportive. I suspect temporary insanity, brought on by stress.

I would also like to thank my illustrious editor, Steve Laube, who had enough faith in me to send me a contract based on nothing more than two sample chapters, and who even gave me an extended deadline, so great was his faith, and who, upon receiving the completed manuscript, shrieked, "You aren't *seriously* planning on putting *that* in the book, are you? *Nyet!!!* Change it now!!! WE ARE AT DEADLINE, YOU LUNATIC!!!"

MORAL: Never put a lot of faith in a humor writer, especially when you have already foolishly sent him a substantial wad of loot and have thus lost a significant amount of leverage.

I must also thank Kris "O Patient One" Landis, the Bethany House website commanderette, who consistently puts up with WAY more from me than I have a right to expect. I feel rather guilty about this, but not guilty enough to actually knock it off. She can at least be grateful that I did not, once again, refer to her in print as Kris "The Cheez Whiz" Landis. Feel free to drop me a thank-you note, Kris!

Mucho appreciation goes to Jeanne Mikkelson, the PR czar, and her trusty assistant Melissa Smith, who tirelessly work to promote my books in the marketplace. How do you two *live* with yourselves?

I serve up a plateful of gratitude as well to Holly Foster, my BHP editorial assistant buddy, who puts up with

ACKNOWLEDGMENTS

all my obsessive pestering and only rarely erupts into a maniacal rage, angrily slamming the phone down and vowing to move to Spain if I ever call again (which I do anyway, sometimes within five minutes).

I direct a big hug to my Aunt Jean, who has always been so enthusiastic about my work and who also suggested that I cover the topic of shopping. Dale will eventually get over it.

Special thanks to Bob and Doris Meurer, my dad and mom, who have been very married for a looong time and who still love each other after all these years and who, when people ask if I am their son, don't even try to deny it. Talk about integrity.

Big thanks go to Carol Johnson, who said yes—once again—to a book proposal by me, thus demonstrating that senior executives of Bethany House Publishers will readily commit two consecutive huge lapses of judgment once you get them giggling. There is a lesson in this, Carol, and I hope you don't learn it.

Lastly, thanks to all the friends, family members, and colleagues who offered suggestions, critiqued the draft, or let me share something from their lives. Your assistance was *invaluable*, which is a clever code word meaning "I am keeping all the money."

Contents

CHAPTER 1

Never Forget the Stuff That Should Be Unforgettable

Oh, c'mon now! Just how many more marriage books do we really need on the market?

How many different ways can different authors re-package essentially the same information, such as: "Avoid name-calling during a conflict" and "It is very important to remember your anniversary" and "Don't keep dredging up the past" (especially when Mr. "On-the-Ball" made last-minute plans to take you both out to *Giff's Ugly Burger* on the Big Day and then ran out of gas on the way, just like last year)?

I say the answer is "at least one more."

Because while most of the other marriage books out there presume that you need to be reminded to remember your anniversary, this is the ONLY book that presumes some of you even need to be reminded that you are *married*.

I do not say this in the haughty, condescending tone

used by many marriage experts. I say this in the compassionate, empathetic tone of someone who once forgot that he was married.

Trust me, you *don't* want to do this.

But because I have "been there," I am uniquely equipped to share special insights, such as, "Boy, will she get her feelings hurt if you forget you are married, even if it is only for a few minutes!"

It isn't like I actually did anything dangerous during that short span in which I forgot we were married. I mean, I wasn't out dating or anything. But you should have seen the look on her face! For Pete's sake, you'd think I had mowed down her favorite flowers or something (which happened *much* later).

(And I *still* say they looked like weeds. Just sort of attractive weeds.)

(How was I supposed to know what a hollyhock is? Anything that tall looks like a weed to me. I majored in journalism, not landscaping.)

But back to the key event.

There is a perfectly good reason why I forgot we were married, as I am sure you will agree if you are a guy and you, too, once forgot you were married. But all the female readers are undoubtedly already getting all sympathetic with my wife and muttering "the DOLT!" under their breath, even though they haven't even heard my side of the story! Talk about an un-Christian, judgmental attitude! Give me a break, ladies! Here I am, spilling my guts in an attempt to help make *your* marriage better, and you are directing all this hostility at me. I can't possibly accomplish the task of helping you improve your nuptial relationship if you are all steamed at me before we even get to the regrettable "sculpture" incident.

But back to the key event. Again.

We had just returned home from our romantic honeymoon to the redwood forest of northern California. It was a warm summer evening, and we were standing out on the balcony of our apartment as we had done on scores of prior occasions back when we were merely engaged.

There had been a certain ritual in our premarriage, end-of-the-day good-bye. We would often linger on the balcony, looking at the stars and talking about life. Before the night got too far gone, I would kiss Dale good-night and send her on her way so she would not run the risk of falling asleep at the wheel on the twenty-minute drive to her home.

Well, old habits die hard. Besides, it was late and I am not an evening person.

We were leaning on the railing, looking out at the courtyard, when I said, as I always eventually said, "Well, we'd better get you on the road home before it gets too late."

As a newly married person, this was not exactly what she was expecting to hear on the very first evening together in our new home.

Yikes! Did she look *surprised!*

"Wha-a-a-t?" she said in a slowly rising tone, with the shocked and bewildered expression you commonly see on the faces of women whose husbands have forgotten they are married.

But I recovered very quickly.

"Oh, that's *right!* We're *married* now! YAHOO!!!"

She forgave me.

Which, at long last, brings me to a **Vital Marriage Point:** Don't accidentally mow down her flowers!

It is one thing to forget (for just a teensy second) that you are married, as there is no lasting damage and, in a way, it actually works out for the better because it re-occurs to you that you now have an official license from God to *seriously* make out. But it is an entirely different story if you mow down her six-foot-high prize flowers, even if you burn rubber down to the store to buy her some replacement seeds.

While she did manage to forgive me, in coming months she would nevertheless often glance out at that bare space in the lawn and ask, "How could you NOT tell they were flowers? They were beautiful!"

Fortunately, life does go on, and she found new things to take her mind off the regrettable hollyhock incident. Unfortunately, one of those "new things" was the regrettable sculpture incident. . . .

What a Wonderful World

We had only been dating for a short while, but as she looked across the crowded room and observed me—hearing my jokes, taking in my amusing mannerisms, and witnessing my childlike exuberance—her thoughts spontaneously turned to marriage.

"I will NEVER marry that man!" she said to herself, and promptly began looking for every plausible excuse to avoid all possible contact with me, while I performed my classic moose imitation during our friends' wedding rehearsal.

Yes, the romantic musings of *"never!"* and *"that man!"* were some of the first thoughts my future spouse had about me; with a heavy emphasis on *"never!"*

But here I am, still "that man" but married to Dale for eighteen blissful years.

How in the world did you two ever go from "never" to "I do"? you may be asking yourself.

Dale is *still* asking that question in her more lucid

moments, which, thankfully, are pretty few these days. I mean, nearly two decades of living with me would just about fry the "lucid" section of any woman's brain. Just ask my sister Jan (but you have to wait until visiting day, and you can't have any sharp objects on your person).

Fortunately, Dale did not have the freedom to act upon her desire to avoid me, because we were both participating in the wedding of our respective roommates, and they politely refused her suggestion to erect a brick wall between us, even though she offered to tastefully cover the aforementioned wall with ivy.

Dale was a bridesmaid for Pam, and I was a groomsman for Tim. And we were in the middle of the wedding rehearsal, where I was practicing my extremely entertaining moose imitation while the minister recited the vows, when Dale made her pledge to *never* be with me, in sickness or in health, and preferably not even in the same hemisphere.

What kind of putz would be doing a moose imitation during a wedding rehearsal? is what she was thinking. *A wedding is the culmination of months and months of planning, and is the biggest thing that will happen in anyone's life. It launches a whole new life together for the happy couple, and the rehearsal is no place for a* stupid *moose imitation!*

Which is precisely why I was doing a *comical* moose imitation instead of the *stupid* rendition, which I save for lesser events, such as golden anniversaries. I have my standards.[1]

So why did Dale eventually marry me?

---

[1] OK, they may not be really *good* standards, but they are still, technically, standards (in the sense that Bangladesh is still, technically, a country).

For much the same reason people listen to Louis Armstrong. They like *other* things about him besides his voice. They like the fact that he was one *fine, fine, **fine*** trumpet player, and they fall in love with his music, and pretty soon that gruff voice grows on them, and pretty soon they actually love it.

I love to lie in a hammock while the outside speakers blare a "Best of Louis Armstrong" CD, where the great "Satchmo" croons, "What a Wonderful World" in his inimitable, gravelly voice.[2] I don't think I would have fallen in love with Louis if he were only a singer. It was that awesome trumpet that got my attention. But the scraggly voice is part of the package deal. He even had the audacity to sing with Bing Crosby, which is just INSANE because nobody has ever crooned like Bing, yet that carefree audacity makes me love Louis even more.

Likewise, Dale was attracted to me for reasons other than my moose imitation. But my fifth-grade sense of humor was part of the package deal. I think she was gambling[3] that I would outgrow it.

There is really no such thing as a match made in heaven. Rather, God has chosen to grant us a match made in Sheboygan, or Minneapolis, or wherever you happen to live. It is all very earthly, with lots of ups and downs, stupid arguments, hurt feelings, and saying, "I'm sorry— would you please forgive me?"

A great marriage is not when the "perfect couple" comes together. It is when an imperfect couple comes

---

[2]Remember when Jesus said that if the Jerusalem crowds ceased shouting His praise, the "stones would cry out"? I think the stones would sound a lot like Louis Armstrong, only more Yiddish.

[3]Clearly, God is using me to help her overcome her gambling problem. You'd think she would be more thankful.

together, crazy for each other, and learns to accommodate, and even come to enjoy, their differences. It is also where God uses each of you to cause growth and maturity.

Which brings me to another **Vital Marriage Point:** Growth and maturity do not necessarily rule out wearing a rubber nose and glasses, a set of which I keep in my closet on the off chance anyone invites me to attend another wedding rehearsal.

I believe that humor props fall under God's rather expansive category of "personal preference," much to Dale's dismay. I am pleased to note also that there is nothing anyone can point to in the Bible that explicitly rules out the use of wind-up chattering teeth. I certainly feel no divine pressure to avoid them.

Conveniently for me, God spends His time and energy working on our character, cultivating qualities like patience, loyalty, kindness, honesty, self-control, and, above all, sacrificial love. He appears to be quite content to let us perform Three Stooges impersonations as long as it isn't during someone's sermon (unless it is a really *bad* sermon, in which case you'd be doing everyone a big favor).

And since Dale already said, "I do," it is too late for her to back out! But she actually doesn't want to back out! In fact, she even laughs at my jokes—occasionally. If I don't go overboard. And if we are not in a wedding party.

Because God is fitting us together, using each other to knock off rough edges, expand our horizons, get one of us to lighten up, and the other one of us to get a grip. I'll leave it to you to figure out who is in what category.

I take great pleasure in the fact that God is using me to help Dale grow as a person. How cool! I get to be a big part of making her a happier, more relaxed, and more ful-filled human being.

And Dale has greatly ministered to me. I am much less moody, much more aware of the feelings and needs of others, and more content and happier today than I was when we were first married.

Being married is kind of like being a missionary to a very tiny tribe of one. You share yourself, you pour out your soul, you bless someone with a deeper and richer understanding of God, but you don't necessarily have to live with gigantic insects or catch malaria. Plus, you both get to lie out in your hammock in the backyard on a warm summer evening and listen to Louis Armstrong.

What a wonderful world!

CHAPTER 3

SEX! (For Men Only)
(This CHAPTER, I Mean, Not Sex Itself!)

One year, possibly in sheer desperation but *definitely* not fully understanding the implications of his actions, the senior pastor of my church put me in charge of the men's ministry. Normally ministers try to get mature and responsible men to fill these key roles. People like, well, *me*, are typically required to first prove themselves in lower-profile tasks, such as stapling the Sunday bulletin. But he apparently mistook me for a spiritually mature person, most likely because he didn't see me and a friend playing "staple war" in the hall.*

Running the men's ministry carried with it the task of setting a theme for the annual men's retreat. I chose "real life" as the topic, not only because I wanted to discuss

---

*"Staple war" is a game wherein the guys who get stuck with bulletin duty shoot staples at each other. The loser is the guy who gets pinned to the church bulletin board. **NOTE:** This game is typically NOT played by Presbyterians.

serious issues that men face in the "real world" but also because this theme is so broad I could cram just about anything into it at the last minute, thus allowing me to procrastinate until the last possible second (which I did).

Someone else was in charge of music, and we ended up singing a little verse that goes, "He's all I need, He's all I need, Jesus is all I need." You just repeat it a few times and it turns into a song.

As we were singing, this little chorus brought back memories of a conversation I had had several years earlier with my two sons, Mark and Brad. We were in church, singing, "He's all I need, He's all I need, Jesus is all I need," when Brad, then eight, leaned over and pointed out, "You need air, too."

"And water," chimed in Mark. "You can only go about two days before you die."

So I conveyed this story to the guys at the retreat.

"My kids were right, really," I said. "But the list of necessities doesn't stop at air and water. Frankly, I'd kind of like to work sex into the mix. This is not easy to do in a song."

Guys emitted stifled, nervous laughter and cast quick looks around the room while I jotted some words on an overhead transparency.

I then laid a song sheet on the projector, and we all sang, in thunderously loud voices:

He's all I need, He's all I need, Jesus and air and water
*and a decent Italian restaurant and sex, is all I need.**

The guys REALLY liked this song. They wanted it in the hymnal.

---

*Yes, we *really* did sing this. The harmony part made it that much more moving.

I mean, face it, we need a LOT of stuff besides God. Just ask Him! After all, God is the one who created the first guy, Adam, and then said, "It is *not* good for man to be alone." Look it up! It's right there in Genesis, chapter 2, verse 18!

God then conked Adam unconscious and created a gorgeous woman for him to have sex with. Not that they ONLY had sex. I mean, they shared a whole life together. Emotions, hopes, dreams, God. But the point still remains that *God himself* was the one who said, in essence, "I'm *not* all he needs." He not only said it, but He also *deliberately* created Adam with physical and emotional longings that God knew He could not fill but Eve could.

God did not create the man and then one day realize, "Whoa! Looks like I accidentally created this guy with a powerful sex drive! Now what will I do?" No, the sex drive was a divine choice. It was planned. It was the way He wanted it to be.

So God does not feel slighted that we need someone other than himself. On the contrary, it is precisely the way He designed us. He intends that we be relational creatures. He especially likes it when we get married, because that is where He can *really* start to work on our character. I think God uses our sexual desire to move us toward commitment, trust, sacrifice, wrenching honesty, and all kinds of stuff you experience in marriage—stuff many males would probably avoid like Tupperware parties were it not for this potent, marvelous craving we call sex.

Rather manipulative of Him, actually.

But it is manipulation in a good way, like when you rock your cranky toddler with the specific intent of lulling him to sleep because he *really* needs a nap. God uses sex to lull us into those other things we *really* need—emotional connectedness, selflessness, loyalty, and excellent cardiovascular exercise.

I was honestly not trying to be irreverent in adding new words to "He's All I Need," and, indeed, I hope I did not offend anyone. But I did it because I believe the typical, subliminal male response to the "He's All I Need" song, and all other songs of that nature, is *guilt*. We wish we were "spiritual" enough to "only" need God, and we sing the song and then—unthinkingly and reflexively—feel guilty that, deep down, we *don't* feel like He is all we need, nor is He all we would *like*.

My sons were the first people I have ever heard say, essentially, "Hey! This song is unrealistic!"

And they were right.

God did *not* put "He's all I need" in the Bible.

God *did* put in the Song of Solomon, which is a bigtime, major-league, doubleheader celebration of sex and romance and the pursuit of a woman by a man. God thinks we guys need a good woman, passion, a soul mate.

I think hymn writers sometimes get carried away with religious verse to the point that it becomes unrealistic, counterproductive, and actually unbiblical.

If God made a perfect, sinless world and a perfect, sinless guy, and put him in a perfect Garden, and regularly visited with the man on a face-to-face basis, but nevertheless said, in effect, "This guy really needs a lover!" who are we to argue? Especially when we can personally verify that the expression of passion—toe-curling, uninhibited, sweaty passion—meets a deep and penetrating need in the very core of our being. It isn't just the physical act, although that, in itself, is a very big deal, but it is the *oneness* of it all. The letting go. The things you say and do for each other that you would only say and do when reduced to that wonderful idiocy of passion.

Sex is a God thing. It is His way of forcing us out of our shell and toward our mate, our Eve, our helper.

I think I helped some guys debunk their guilt with that modified song, but I probably also *seriously* stepped over some lines that had never been stepped over—like altering a church song to include not only sex but also really good ethnic food. Well, that's what you get when you take someone like me out of the staple brigade and put him in charge of a men's ministry. Which only goes to prove that when it comes to men's ministry leadership, I'm definitely *not* all you need.

Cold Feet

We live in the northern Central Valley of California, where in summer months we experience temperatures so high that your spleen sweats. It is not unusual for our town to make national news for being the hottest place in the country, surpassing several desert locations and even a few pizza ovens. If you have never experienced a 115-degree day, you can somewhat replicate the experience by pointing sixteen hair dryers at your face, all on the MAXIMUM FRY setting, while you sit in the engine compartment of a 1964 Chevy Impala, which is being unmercifully revved by the irritating seventeen-year-old kid who lives down the street.*

We did not end up in this barbecue by accident. On the contrary, I deliberately shopped around for weather so preposterously parched, so hideously blistering, so unbelievably sizzling that it would give a scorpion heat

---

*Note to personal injury attorneys: I am not actually suggesting that anyone try this, so save the lawsuits.

prostration. If Venus, which has a surface temperature exceeding a commercial clothes dryer, had breathable air and accepted credit cards, I would have purchased a home there eighteen years ago. The northern Central Valley of California was the next best thing.

This does not mean that I dislike winter. Actually, I enjoy Jack Frost nipping at my exposed facial appendages. Winter means snowball fights and the welcoming glow of the fireplace and not mowing the lawn.

But it takes the thermal blast of a northern California summer to thaw out my wife's otherwise perpetually frozen feet. And I am by no means the only husband in this predicament. Scientific studies have demonstrated that while some men get cold feet on the day of their wedding, women (particularly of Swedish descent) live in a perpetual podiatric ice age. And simply cranking up the thermostat to the high eighties will not melt the twin glaciers concealed in those Eddie Bauer fleece-lined, down-filled slippers.

No, the only lasting relief available comes from several months of toe-defrosting summer heat. But until June rolls around, these desperate women in their quest for warmth will seek what relief they can in the middle of a bitter winter's night by rubbing their icy feet all over the legs of the hapless soul who promised before God and the assembled witnesses that he would be with her for richer, for poorer, for warmer, for colder.

Believe me, I have tried alternatives. Hot water bottles are OK until the water turns to ice. Ironing the sheets before my parka-clad wife leaped into bed only bought about nine seconds of peace. Stacking four electric blankets one on top of the other not only set the bed on fire but also brought a rather shrill rebuke from the fire marshal.

Yet according to my wife, not even a dozen electric blankets can thaw her frozen corpuscles like *my legs* can. So I shiver and suffer and pray for the searing days of summer.

As you can imagine, this state of affairs puts a real damper on the idea of romantic winter evenings together. Let's face it, by the time your beloved pulls on three pairs of wool socks, two pairs of sweat pants, a flannel nightgown, and a knit ski cap, we are basically talking about the romance factor of an Egyptian mummy.

Some men simply come up with thinly veiled excuses to never come to bed during the winter. Mill workers, for example, have come to blows over the right to work the graveyard shift. Others walk through bad parts of town, hoping that a good mugging will give them amnesia and they will be unable to remember their address for a few months.

Prior to getting married, I often wondered how in the world those tough macho hombre guys who sit motionless for hours in the predawn frozen confines of a duck blind, or stand hip deep in a 36-degree stream while lashing the surface with a fly line, can *stand* it. It is now clear that the cowards are simply escaping to a more temperate climate. While it certainly isn't any picnic to have a big, stupid labrador retriever shake freezing pond water all over you at five o'clock in the morning, at least Ginger doesn't rub her icy paws all over your bare legs (possibly because she sees that you have a shotgun).

The nonhunting male, on the other hand, is driven to equally pathetic stunts, such as hiding in the basement and hoping his wife won't notice that the shapeless lump under the covers on his side of the bed is actually the toaster wrapped in their son's *Bugs Bunny* sleeping bag.

Not that I have ever stooped to such outlandish attempts at self-preservation. No, my rat-fink friend Tim stole my idea before I could try it out, and the way this Siberian sisterhood network works, a good idea is quickly exposed and thus rendered useless.

So, gentlemen, I'll meet you at the duck blind at 4:00 A.M.

CHAPTER 5

Babies!

Great Scott! An entire chapter ago I wrote about sex, and it *just occurred* to me that, up until now, I forgot that sex, in addition to being *loads* of quivering, gasping fun, also just so happens to be the means by which God has chosen to propagate the human race. I was so caught up in the fun of the subject that I temporarily forgot that sex can result in babies, which is *precisely* the kind of mental lapse millions of googly-eyed couples experience on a regular basis, which helps explain why our nation has an ever-growing number of new Toys R Us stores.

There is an inverse relationship between our romance level and our intelligence quotient. On a graph, it looks like the following:

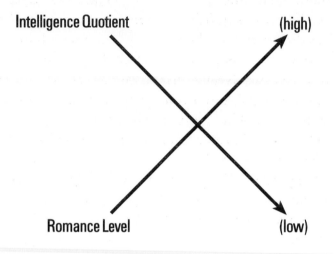

Intelligence Quotient   (high)

Romance Level   (low)

Thus it is entirely possible for a brilliant professor of human anatomy, who received the Nobel Prize for his insightful research into the human reproductive system, to be romantically involved with his wife one evening and decide that he does not want to interrupt the bliss of the moment while they fiddle with some contraceptive option, so he will say, "We won't get pregnant this time."

He has absolutely **NOTHING** scientific upon which to base his declaration. And neither did YOU when YOU said it! But even though we know how our bodies work, fully aware that during our romantic event, the "U.S. Male" express delivers several million highly energetic and single-minded cells *who are excellent swimmers* and who are in a cellular version of a freestyle Olympic race to see who wins the Gold Medal and thus gets to become your next little bundle of joy, we choose to *completely ignore reality*.

Now, what kind of God would create intelligent and rational creatures, loftily made in the very image of himself, and then imbue them with a powerful impulse that can rapidly turn them into the mental equivalent of scrap iron? The answer is, obviously, the kind of God who wants many more of us! And if you will look at population demographics, His plan is certainly working!

When He told Adam and Eve to "be fruitful and multiply and fill the earth," He didn't have to repeat those marching orders! They happily and busily went to work complying, probably day and night, at every opportunity. And we have all been complying ever since.

If procreation were a lot of drudgery and hard work and required wads of self-motivation, like when you remodel your kitchen or read *War and Peace*, you would probably be able to fit the entire human race into downtown Chattanooga. But God has purposefully created a system in which the end result of the most exhilarating possible activity on the planet often results in children. Even when people try a variety of means to enjoy all this fun without winding up with the logical pitter-patter of little feet, they often fail. Your reproductive system is smarter than you are. And those little cells with tails are WAY more motivated than you are. So it may take a while, but the more chances you give them, the higher the likelihood they will eventually succeed.

I am not trying to say that most children result from a passion-induced lapse of memory, although there *is* quite a bit of that. On the contrary, even when we are not filled with the ardor of the moment, God gives us a longing to have children. He has put something in our very core that longs to reproduce. This longing pretty much goes with life. As we look around the world God has made, we see that (1) life wants to live; (2) life wants to make more of itself; and (3) life will do this whether or not the child tax credit is increased.

All life has an innate need to "reproduce after its own kind." I am just saying it is a good thing God made the initial process of having children a ton of fun or there would be a whole lot fewer of them. While, conceptually, I have always wanted children, there are also other things I have always conceptually wanted, such as a totally buff body and biceps the size of a Chevy. I also wish I could run a marathon and be on the National Diving Team. I wish I were the very model of virile health.

But working out is not fun. It is *work*, hence the term "working out," and it is more work than I am willing to devote in order to obtain the desired end. So my kids are very fortunate that a grueling fitness regime or the ability to put up wallpaper was not a prerequisite to their conception, or they would probably not be here to smell the roses and ask me for money.

As is always the case, God knew what He was doing. There was no way He was going to predicate the existence of future generations on our willingness to perform a grim, unpleasant, and difficult task. No, He made sex sheer brainless pleasure to make sure we would engage in it, and He reserved the "grim, unpleasant, and difficult" stuff for later (specifically, *childbirth* and, lest you dads think you will get off scot-free, *diapers*).

It is a testimony to the creative genius of God that He could make sex so wonderfully gratifying that it can even overcome a woman's aversion to fifteen hours worth of labor pains, a man's reflexive dread of diapers, and even the combined intellect of both husband and wife. In fact, even as I sit here writing about the delight of sex weighed against the costs, listening to my wife singing in the shower, with the dawning realization that our kids are away at summer camp so we have the house to ourselves, I can almost sense my IQ dipping . . . dropping . . . falling to dangerissly loe levvells.

I'm sure we won't get pregnant this time. . . .

CHAPTER 6

Waking Up Is Hard to Do
-or-
"Thar She Blows"

Waking up next to a pregnant woman is like waking up next to a motion-detecting bomb. You really, *really* can't afford one false move.

Have you ever seen one of those movies where the insane villain holds the damsel-in-distress hostage by strapping an explosive device to her body? If she so much as twitches—KABOOM!

That's where the brave hero comes in and, risking his own life, rescues her.

With a pregnancy, the husband gets to play the role of *both* the insane villain and the brave hero. The plot is simple: he got her into this mess, and he had better rescue her.

When my wife, Dale, was pregnant for the first time, she woke up horribly nauseous one morning. She desperately wanted a saltine cracker, but I did not know this because she was so queasy she could only manage to moan, "Crerr."

Well, "crerr" is not a word I recognized.

"What?" I asked.

"Crerr!" she whispered, frozen in place, with a desperate look on her brow.

"Do you want me to get you something?" I asked.

"Crerr," she nodded, ever so slightly.

"Bacon and eggs OK?"

"KABOOM!" went the hostage.

She later explained—rather testily—that "crerr" means, "I want you to get me a cracker and some warm tea **IMMEDIATELY** before I get violently ill, but you need to ease out of bed very **s-l-o-w-l-y** so you don't jostle me."

Regrettably, there is an inherent contradiction in the directive to do something both "immediately" and "slowly." So we had a few more KABOOMS until I at least "sort of" mastered the technique, which was (1) levitate out of bed without so much as brushing against a sheet molecule; (2) make a cup of mild tea, with just three granules of sugar to take out the bitterness; and (3) have both the tea and the cracker ready for her the split second she wakes up.

As you can imagine, these were tense mornings.

Besides, I think it is a pretty big deal for the hero to rescue the damsel *once*—but EVERY SINGLE DAY for three solid months?

You remember our good friends Tim and Pam. Pam was likewise stricken with morning sickness—only it was more like "morning, afternoon, and evening sickness."

"At first I was right by her side every time she ran for the bathroom," Tim told me. "I would get her a glass of water and a washcloth and pat her back and practically be in tears, I felt so bad for her."

But as time wore on, he found himself just calling out, "You doing OK in there?"

Toward the end, this devolved into Tim remarking, "Hey, try not to spill my nachos!" as Pam bolted from the bed and dove for the porcelain target.

Tim would just continue watching TV or reading his book.

Now, it isn't that guys are insensitive Neanderthals, it's just that the routine starts to get a little old after awhile. Besides, it isn't like we can make our wives feel better anyway. I mean, if we *could* we certainly *would*, but even with the tea and crackers and all our best efforts, the odds are that Old Faithful is going to blow sky-high anyway. So we guys tend to get a little fatalistic.

But even if I survived the daily morning disarmament drill, I was by no means home free. Pregnancy does REALLY weird things to a woman, including, in Dale's case, creating an insatiable need for stir-fried cabbage at nine o'clock at night. Nothing else would do. And she wanted it NOW!

So I would speed to the store to buy enough cabbage to feed an entire convention of vegetarians. But the next night, cabbage was out and zucchini was in. Menu planning was impossible. The clock would strike nine, and only then would the mystery craving be revealed—and it was almost always some offbeat substance that we did not have readily available in the cupboard, such as steamed paprika on rye.

I have never heard an adequate explanation for the bizarre food desires of pregnant women. Not that I doubt for a moment that these wild desires are real. On the contrary, they are a staple of pregnant-woman lore through the centuries. But WHY?

Aside from the obvious fact that her body is seeking certain nutrients to keep the developing baby healthy, I have a hunch that this is yet another one of those "God things"—like making sure our babies require diaper assistance when He could have just as easily let them take in carbon dioxide and give off oxygen like your basic Boston fern.*

Pregnant animals don't ask for special diets. Mrs. Lion doesn't say to Mr. Lion, "Yuck! Keep that dead wildebeest away from me and get me a peach yogurt!"

No, animals just keep eating the same old thing they've always eaten.

But women turn into moody, weepy, goofy, sleepy, irritable insomniacs with food allergies—sometimes all in the space of five minutes. The net result is that guys are given the opportunity to be *more* supportive, *more* understanding, *more* patient, *more* protective, and *more* loving than ever before. Which, of course, is precisely what God wants from us anyway, so it only increases my suspicion that this state of affairs is not simply a coincidence.

Further bolstering my "God-thing" theory is the fact that infants *also* tend to be moody, weepy, goofy, sleepy, irritable insomniacs with food allergies! So it looks very much like God has arranged pregnancy as a sort of parenthood "boot camp," except that the person who even-

---

*Read more about this theory in my first book, *Boyhood Daze*.

tually yells at you at four o'clock in the morning at the top of his lungs is much shorter than a typical drill sergeant, plus he has a wet diaper.

The truly amazing thing about pregnancy is that, even with all its inherent dangers and difficulties, most men survive it.

CHAPTER 7

Thanks for the Mammaries

In this chapter we are going to discuss feeding your infant, which means that we are going to be treading on *very* sensitive ground because I must come right out and mention—in a book that is being distributed by a *Christian* publisher—the Infant Beverage Conveyance System.

Christian publishers are *notoriously* bashful when discussing any sector of the human body that is not used exclusively for breathing, hearing, speaking, walking, writing, or blinking.

A fellow author told me that some Christian publishers are only willing to discuss the sectors of the body that "God made." And those sectors are restricted to whatever can be seen while you are seated in church. (We aren't talking here about one of those "indigenous churches" in a so-called "developing nation." As the official Christian Publisher Motto states, "Everybody knows that '*indigenous*' is just a fancy word for '*naked*.'")

This editorial unwillingness to use plain words and

acknowledge the obvious results in some incredibly comical and uptight reading material.

Dale and I received as a wedding present a book about the Song of Solomon, which is the Bible's celebration of love and passion.

But this particular book began with the stern and dour warning that the Song of Solomon was ONLY an ALLEGORY concerning God's love for people and had NOTHING to do with ANYTHING that you young people might be THINKING it has to do with.

This book was given to us by an elderly person.

This book cracked me up!

The author had to literally *torture* the English language with a cattle prod to come up with absolutely *ludicrous* metaphors about the meaning of chapter 4, verse 5. (Look it up for yourself. My uptight editor won't let me quote it.)

I would LOVE to read that author's attempt at a romance novel:

"Charles gently grasped the hand of his new bride, dreaming of the evening to come when all their longing and expectation would be met in that special moment when they opened the Matthew Henry Commentary on Leviticus."

But, of course, that author would never even order "stuffed chicken torso" at a restaurant much less write a romance novel.

I am not that kind of strict and rigid writer. I realize that in order to be relevant to the contemporary reader I must frankly discuss, with no awkwardness or hesitation, the many important issues surrounding the debate over "the bottle" as opposed to—and I will be blunt here—"the other method."

The following comparison chart, complete with a fair and impartial scoring system that rates each category, will help you flesh out (so to speak) the merits of each option and then make a sound decision:

The Formula & Bottle Method vs. The Opposite of That

Formula & Bottle	Score	Opposite of That	Score
Costs a lot of money	1	Free	5
Requires extensive preparation	1	Immediate	5
Requires a stove or a microwave	1	Nada	5
Can be lost or misplaced	1	Never	5
Can be too hot or too cold	1	Always perfect	5
Considered acceptable by doctors	3	Preferred by doctors	5
Either parent can perform the task	5	Dad is home free!	50,000
TOTAL	13	**TOTAL**	50,030

Let's do a quick tally and—whoa! Looks like there's no contest here!

Nursing is clearly the better option from the standpoint of economics, practicality, and nutrition—and it just so happens that the father is *completely out of the loop*! Is this a God thing or what? I feel positively *worshipful*!

At this point in the writing of this manuscript, my wife looked over my shoulder and made the following observation:

"You're right, Dave! God has arranged it so the mom can be rocking her baby while nursing and bonding, and the dad is free to wash the dishes, or cook, or vacuum, or change the toddler's diaper, or any one of a hundred other possibilities! That was certainly thoughtful of Him!"

Hmm . . .

So we may have to shave a few thousand points off the score.

Nevertheless, strong arguments still remain for nursing. For example, a nursing baby is essentially a small human Hoovermatic who literally whisks calories from a woman's body—and at a 100 percent discount off the price charged by Weight Watchers. This is a big plus for women, who are often deeply concerned about how much weight they gained during pregnancy—not that we, as husbands, noticed *any* weight gain whatsoever, and we absolutely *refuse* to comment any further, because we have learned that while it is perfectly acceptable for women to discuss this issue among themselves, it is perilous if men touch the subject with a 300-foot pole.

EXAMPLE:

PREGNANT WOMAN #1: "I can't believe I've put on thirty-nine pounds. I feel like a blimp. How about you?"

PREGNANT WOMAN #2: "Forty-five pounds. It's awful. I feel like one of those huge sea lions you see on those nature shows."(They laugh together.)

CLUELESS GUY: "I guess it *is* pretty amazing how much weight women put on during pregnancy."

PREGNANT WOMAN #1: "How DARE you, you insensitive BRUTE!"

PREGNANT WOMAN #2: "SHOOT HIM!"
(**NOTE TO CLUELESS GUYS:** Pregnancy is an emotional minefield. We will explore this subject further
in my upcoming book titled *How to Not Lose Your Limbs
and Valuable Internal Organs in the Emotional Minefield*.
But back to the subject at hand.)

Even with all the advantages, there are a few down-
sides to God's handy patented lactose-dispensing
method. For one thing, it is very difficult for Mom to get
out of the house alone to get a break and some needed
downtime. The tike could wake up hungry at any moment, and Dad would be floundering around trying to
sing to him and bounce him and generally make a failing
attempt to distract the infant from the fact that he is hungry. Men are horrified at the prospect of being left home
with a crying baby whose most basic need we cannot fill.

Fortunately, there is an ingenious beverage extraction
and storage device on the market that can help solve this
problem, thus permitting Mom and Dad to go to a restaurant alone on occasion while Grandma baby-sits, and
we men are so grateful for this device that there is no way
we are going to point out that it is essentially a miniature
version of what you would find in a commercial dairy operation (but without the three-legged stool).

The other significant issues regarding infant dietary
habits have to do with timing (babies have *zero* sense of
timing) and noise (based on their personality and level of
hunger, nursing babies can perfectly imitate the sound
created by a ten-year-old who is consuming the last drop
of his milk shake by inhaling it through a straw at a wind
speed of sixty-five miles per hour).

Thus Mom and Dad can be in a social situation, such as playing Scrabble with friends, and the little guy decides he is hungry. Now, a *really smooth* mom can so quickly and discreetly maneuver her baby into "dinner mode"—not even missing her chance to play the eighty-seven-point word "Jacuzzi"—that you don't even realize the kid is happily nursing away. A particularly adept mother could probably get away with even more complex activities, such as starring in a Broadway play. But that only lasts until **SLURRRP!**

Discretion is not in your baby's vocabulary. Come to think of it, NOTHING is in your baby's vocabulary, except "Burp," "Goo," and "Waah!" So no matter how modest and discreet the mom tries to be, she can't count on a great deal of help from the baby. After all, this is the same kid who will spit up on anyone who happens to be holding him at the opportune time. Of course, even former President Bush once "lost it" on the prime minister of Japan, so your kid is not really pushing the envelope all that much when he has a little "oops" on whoever is patting him on the back.

And most people are very understanding and forgiving, because babies are simply adorable. Adults are keenly aware—sometimes painfully so—that infancy only lasts for a very, *very*, **very** little while.

There were times when Mark was quite young that Dale and I were so exhausted it seemed like the "helpless stage" would last forever. Dale was sore from nursing and deeply tired from the nighttime feedings. I was fried from my own support activities, including rocking a cranky, sick little Mark to sleep at 2:00 A.M. I sometimes wondered when it would end.

The answer turned out to be "too soon."

Many doctors recommend nursing for at least the baby's first year. But long before the weaning process begins, you will introduce your baby to other foods. (It may be pulverized beyond recognition, but according to the FDA it is still legally "food.") What neither you nor your baby realize at the time is that with that very first spoonful of strained applesauce he is on the road to growing up. He is on the path—strike that—he is on the *freeway* to toddlerhood, which will rapidly lead to preschool, then real school—with grades and homework and awkwardness and dating and sports and big life decisions—then college or vocational training and a job and responsibility and marriage and a tiny baby of his own who nurses in peace and dozes off nestled next to Mommy.

And the first tiny step toward independence is taken when he graduates from "Mommy only." Your little baby is going to someday be on his own in a world that can be unfair, unkind, and fraught with the frightening possibility of seeing old *Brady Bunch* episodes on cable.

It would certainly be easier to stay a baby and have someone else care for your every need. But God does not give us that option. We are destined to be weaned, because we are destined to grow.

> But I have stilled and quieted my soul;
> like a weaned child with its mother,
> like a weaned child is my soul within me.
> —Psalm 131:2

CHAPTER 8

Alien Impostor Boys

During my entire childhood it seemed like my mom was perpetually astonished by the fact that I was growing up. I would walk into the house after kindergarten—or third grade, or high school—and she would, on a regular basis, stare at me wide-eyed and say something like, "I just can't believe how *tall* you are getting! It seems like just *yesterday* you were a toddler!"

And I would reply, "So what do you want me to do, shrink?"

And she would just shake her head and walk away, still making incredulous comments.

One day as a high school sophomore, I came into the house, and Mom was—once again—absolutely *shocked* by my appearance. She gaped at me and appeared ready to faint. You'd think I had grown a third nostril or something.

"Why, it seems like just yesterday you were eating paste in Mrs. Marshall's kindergarten class! What happened to you?" she exclaimed, shaking her head.

I was exasperated.

"Mom, you just saw me this morning! I haven't grown any observable amount today! What is so surprising?"

I could never understand why Mom would get all weepy and sentimental about a simple biological process. Living things grow. This is natural. Kids get bigger. So what?

But from the way she talked about it, you'd think someone had slipped her a Rip Van Winkle pill and she'd spent years at a time in a coma, awakening just often enough to be amazed at how much her children had changed since she dozed off during the Lyndon Johnson administration.

I, on the other hand, was champing at the bit to make time move even faster so I could get a driver's license and then graduate from high school and move on to college and be independent and start to really live my life. Time was already moving too slowly as far as I was concerned, but it almost seemed like Mom wanted the clock to stand still completely.

"You just won't understand until you have children of your own," Mom said.

I finally got to test her hypothesis when I married Dale and became the father of Mark and Brad. One day as I left for work, Mark was just starting to take his first tentative steps. He would crawl over to the couch, clutch the cushions with his tiny hands, pull himself up, and then take unsteady strides as he hugged the furniture for balance. Dale and I clapped and gave him encouragement, and I could hardly wait to get home so I could see his progress. Unlike my misty-eyed, hopelessly sentimental mom, I welcomed the advances of each new day as a normal part of the growth process.

I finally arrived home, eager to play our favorite game of "horsey ride," where I would bounce Mark on my leg while holding his hands. And I was really looking forward to seeing how his walking had improved in my absence.

I walked in the door and called out, "I'm home!"

Typically Mark would come crawling excitedly down the hall, leaving behind a trail of drool. But this time he *walked* right into the living room with no hesitation at all.

"Hi, Dad. Can you take me and Kyle to the mall?" he asked.

"AAIIIEEEEEEE!" I shrieked.

Mark jumped back in alarm.

"What's wrong?" he asked, concern etched in his Clearasil-laden brow.

"WHAT HAPPENED TO YOU?!" I shouted. "You were just barely starting to walk, and now you are a TEENAGER and you are asking for a ride to the MALL!!!"

Mark sighed. "Please, not that again. You and Mom have gotten so weird ever since I started driver's education."

"AAIIIEEEEEEE!" I shrieked again. "How long have I been in a coma? You can't be learning to drive! You're supposed to be a baby!!! We were supposed to play horsey ride!!!"

"On second thought, I think I'll walk to the mall," Mark replied, edging toward the door.

"You aren't going ANYWHERE until you eat a jar of paste!" I barked, as I rummaged through my office.

But when I turned around, he was gone.

I ran down the hall to find Dale, but bumped into yet another teen boy who had the faint beginnings of a mustache.

"Hi, Dad. Can you sign the form for my high school electives courses for next year? I was thinking of taking Spanish."

"AAIIIEEEEEEE!" I howled, barreling down the hall.

"You prefer French, apparently," he called after me as I locked myself in our bedroom, where Dale was putting away some clothes.

"You need to brace yourself, hon," I said, gripping her hands in mine. "Something bizarre and unearthly has happened. Something right out of a science fiction movie. Something too strange to be true."

Dale looked at me intently, then said, "So you actually remembered to write down an ATM transaction?"

"This is no time for joking," I snapped. "We turned our backs for a moment and our kids have been transformed into giants! They are supposed to be using crayons and riding tricycles, and instead they are taking driver's education courses and growing more body hair than KoKo the Gorilla! Something has happened to our little boys!"

"Well, they can't stay young forever," Dale replied, smiling.

"THEY DIDN'T STAY YOUNG FOR THREE MONTHS!" I shot back. "Something has gone horribly wrong! Maybe I have been a guinea pig in a secret government experiment! Or maybe our kids were abducted by aliens, and these are alien impostor boys!"

"I think someone needs a glass of warm milk and a nap," Dale replied.

She was clearly in denial, poor soul. So I did what any

mature male would do when confronted by such a terrifying phenomenon. I called my mom.

"Mom, something weird and inexplicable has happened," I began. "Our kids have sprouted up overnight like beanstalks on steroids! It's unnatural! At the rate they're growing, within three weeks they'll make Michael Jordan look like one of the Seven Dwarves!"

"Well, I always said you would understand someday," she replied, laughing. "It happens so fast. This is just like when you were growing up."

"NO, IT ISN'T!" I cried. "I think they're ALIENS! Can't you see? Put it all together! Bizarre, unearthly growth patterns! And that unintelligible music they listen to! It's a secret alien code from the Mother Ship! Aliens have abducted our sweet little toddlers and replaced them with creatures from the planet Zitlot 5. They are eating us out of house and home, sucking up all the hot water for their abnormally long showers, and even making us pay for their basketball shoes! It is a huge interstellar scam and we are the victims! I want my babies back! I want to play horsey and take them on piggyback rides and read *Green Eggs and Ham* and watch them battle the pediatrician!"

Mom let me finish my tirade before she spoke.

"Now you understand what I meant when I kept telling you how fast time was flying," she said. "But what I didn't know back then, and what I will share with you now, is that there actually is a way to turn back the clock and recapture those days. So don't panic. I'll let you in on the secret."

"Well?" I asked impatiently.

She paused.

"Grandchildren," she replied.

I can hardly wait. I just wish time could move faster. . . .

CHAPTER 9

A Truly Alarming Trend

Every few years or so a nonprofit public interest group staffed by scholarly and dedicated alarmist whiners publishes an "alarming finding" to the effect that we are all in GRAVE DANGER because of (1) something we really like, such as a Big Mac; or (2) something we have no control over, such as a planet-pulverizing asteroid larger than Senator Kennedy.

These groups NEVER warn us about the grim danger posed by things we already DON'T like and are studiously avoiding anyway, such as tofu burgers and yappy little poodles.

But what really bugs me is that these overgrown hall monitors always seem to miss the *truly* frightful and ominous trends, such as the recent upsurge in the percentage of young people who are experimenting with '70s music.

While I do not wish to create any undue panic among those of you who personally lived through the '70s, simple human decency compels me to point out that legions of acne-enhanced adolescents who have tired of rap and ska and other modern permutations of music are deliberately and on a regular basis tuning into "oldies" FM stations where they run the alarming possibility of hearing "Billy, Don't Be a Hero," "Baby, Baby, Don't Get Hooked on Me," and even—brace yourself—"Kung Fu Fighting."

If you reacted to the previous paragraph with an alarmed sharp intake of breath, followed by one or more of those songs spontaneously erupting in the sector of your brain that you desperately hoped and prayed would never awaken from its slumber,

"BILLY, don't be a HERO . . ." and now, even though you are a law-abiding, churchgoing citizen, you are seized by an almost pathological urge to VIOLENTLY MAIM those recording artists, and you are tempted to pummel me for even MENTIONING those AWFUL songs that are now playing over and over and over again like an endless eight-track cartridge jammed into the JVC tape deck of your mind,

"BABY, BABY, don't get hooked on ME . . ." then you see why I am so alarmed about this

"Everybody was KUNG FU fighting . . ." alarming trend.

Dale and I first stumbled onto this alarming trend one night as our teenage son Mark sat at the dining room table doing his homework and humming "Do the Hustle." We had not heard "Do the Hustle" for nearly twenty years, and we greeted its comeback with all the enthusiasm you would feel if you were groping in the refrigerator for a late-night snack and you inadvertently plunged your hand into a twenty-year-old bowl of moldy, pulsing tapioca pudding hidden at the back of the shelf.

"Where did you hear THAT?" I asked, my voice rising into soprano range.

"Youth group," Mark replied. "Justin was whistling it. He does it all the time. I think he heard it on the 'oldies' station. It kind of sticks with you."

"Like a leech," said Dale.

"Like shrapnel in your gut," I added.

"Like disco DNA embedded in every single cell in your body," ventured Dale.

It would have been bad enough if our son had picked up this awful tune through some kind of tragic accident, such as the misfire of secret CIA weapons designed to blast disco music particles right into the cerebral cortex of enemy agents. But Mark was actually picking this stuff up AT A CHURCH FUNCTION!

I tried to gently inform the youth pastor, Ted, about our concerns:

"Ted, I'd like to begin by underscoring that you are doing a great job as youth pastor," I said, carefully projecting a warm and sincere smile. "However, if Mark comes home humming any more disco music, or any other music from the '70s, I will bludgeon you into a stupor with a stack of Captain & Tennille records. DO YOU KNOW WHAT RECORDS ARE? AND DO I MAKE MYSELF CLEAR, OR DO I NEED TO EMPLOY A LITTLE KUNG FU FIGHTING?"

Alas, it was too late. Dozens of kids had rediscovered the 1970s, so the genie was already out of the *I Dream of Jeannie* bottle. They were infected with tunes ranging from Paul McCartney's incredibly stupid "Someone's Knockin' at the Door," which consists entirely of the aging Beatle crooning that someone really should open the door because someone is knocking on it (duh!), to some other guy singing about riding through the desert on a horse with no name, which includes the observation that it is nice to be out of the rain (duh!) and that, for some odd reason, in the desert you can remember your name for there ain't no one for to give you no pain.

What did those songs MEAN, anyway?

If some guy found himself riding through the desert on a horse with no name, why wouldn't he just NAME THE HORSE? And why can't this guy remember his own name unless he is in the desert? And is there some connection here with a movie titled *A Man Called Horse,* which I have never seen but which I am pretty sure was ALSO made in the '70s and which would sort of tie these mysteries together (in a stupid sort of way)?

OFFICER: I am afraid I have to cite you for speeding through the desert on this horse with no name. What's your name, sir?

VOCAL ARTIST: Horse.

OFFICER: Well, it's the '70s, so I guess this somehow makes sense.

VOCAL ARTIST: Regrettably, I can only remember my name when I am in the desert, where there ain't no one for to give me no pain.

OFFICER: Then I'm afraid I'll have to cite you for bad grammar.

JUDGE: I sentence the vocal artist to thirty days of Barry Manilow singing "Mandy."

VOCAL ARTIST: Can I have a lethal injection instead?

So you can see why it is hard for us to get all worked up about theoretical dangers such as the ozone hole, when we are facing very tangible hazards such as the possibility of hearing "Torn Between Two Lovers," which is THE WORST song ever emitted in the 1970s.

Unless we are also counting "Having My Baby."

Or "Feelings."

Or EVERY SINGLE SONG ever squeaked by the Bee Gees.

Maybe Dale and I will just escape to the desert on a horse with no name, where there ain't no radio for to give us no pain.

CHAPTER 10

The Content of Her Character

"The boys need to be at school extra early tomorrow for that project," I mentioned casually to Dale one evening as we were getting into bed. "Plus, the weather report says we are going to have a nasty storm first thing. Fortunately for you, I am going to be the thoughtful and compassionate husband in the morning."

"Thanks, hon," she grinned.

"Don't mention it," I replied.

Unusually alert considering the lateness of the hour, Dale immediately noticed that the alarm clock had been moved to her side of the bed.

"What is *this* doing here?" she asked suspiciously.

"Like I said, the kids have to go to school early," I replied.

"You just told me YOU were going to take them!" she retorted.

"No, I said I was going to be thoughtful and compassionate," I corrected. "Part of being a good husband is

65

doing what is in the best interest of your spouse. I'm just trying to be helpful.''

"I am completely confused," Dale replied. "Are you saying you *are* or are *not* planning to take the kids to school?''

"Hon, I would love to drive the kids to school. But as husbands and fathers, we men have a special obligation to the character development of our families. Like it or not, God has given us this role. I think getting up early to take the kids will help develop your character. I am willing to give up this valuable character-building opportunity so that you can grow as a person," I explained.

"Oh, *now* I get it," she replied, slapping her hand on her forehead. "This is all for *my* own good! And heaven knows *you* don't need any character development! Why, you have more character in your left ear than I have in my entire body! You are a walking festival of character! A veritable character factory, belching excess virtue out of your character smokestack!''

I blushed at the flattery.

"Well, I don't know if I'd go *quite* that far, but you are getting the general idea," I said.

"Oh, but I've only just begun!" she exclaimed. "You have so much surplus character that you could ship it to India and dole it out to underprivileged children! We could sell your superfluous character by the pound at huge discount warehouses! Soon the entire nation will be awash in all the extra character you have been wasting all these years!''

"Dale, if I didn't know you better, I would suspect you are getting a little bit sarcastic," I said suspiciously.

"Not at all," she replied. "Your extra character is the

talk of the town. In fact, at church last week Pastor Paul came up to me and asked, 'How do you manage to *live* with that character?' "

"You know, I could take that two ways," I mused.

"You can figure out which way he meant it as you drive the kids to school tomorrow," she replied, handing me the alarm clock.

Vital Marriage Point: Some women are very resistant to character development.

CHAPTER 11

And MORE About SEX!

One common stereotype women have of men is that we are obsessed with sex. For example, just because this book has already featured two chapters that are about sex, and because this chapter is also about sex, and because I tried to get away with two more chapters about sex until my unamused editor began yelling at me, many women, such as my wife, are thinking, "Good grief! Is he obsessed with sex or what?"

What an unfair stereotype! But even as women are unfairly caricaturing us guys as having the sex drive of hyperactive weasels,[1] we men are quietly going about the daily business of doing our jobs, taking care of the lawn, paying bills, getting the tires rotated, and engaging in a host of other productive activities, in many cases going an *entire five minutes* without thinking about sex, which proves we are not obsessed with this topic, but merely

[1]For the record, the *Journal of the American Medical Association* has documented that men have the sex drive of hyperactive *ferrets*, not weasels. So there.

very, very interested in it. (That's "very" to the twenty-fourth power.)

This high level of interest in sex is largely due to biological factors, and thus we guys could not change our colossal fascination with sex even if we wanted to, which we most certainly *don't*, because we really *like* being this way. It's fun! Just ask us! (If you happen to be married to us, that is!)

None of this is meant to imply that men *enjoy* sex more than women do. That is not at all the case. It's just that men *think* about sex so much more than women do, and men are also genetically designed to become amorous at a much lower threshold.

EXAMPLE: If a husband and wife can get free of the kids for an evening and have a nice candlelight dinner out at their favorite establishment and then have a long, lingering discussion about life over coffee, there is a high degree of likelihood that the woman is going to be fully prepared to engage in an evening of passion. While the guy will also be prepared for a romantic interlude, the fact is he was prepared for it HOURS ago when he stopped by the store on an errand to pick up some laundry soap, because the soap reminded him of bubbles, and the bubbles reminded him of the time they took that bubble bath together in the Jacuzzi tub, and—ZING!!!—he screeches into the driveway whistling, "I'm in the Mood for Love."

But women do not typically find purchasing cleaning products to be a deeply moving, sensual experience, even if we are talking about those cleaning products that feature the words "bold" or "enzyme action." And that is one of the key differences between the genders. Because the guy picks up the package and thinks, "Man, would I love to engage in some bold enzyme action when I get home," even though that phrase makes NO SENSE whatsoever. But as I noted in a prior chapter, sexual arousal precisely corresponds with a marked drop in our intelligence quotient. Fortunately, this phenomenon applies to both men and women. So while guys get stupider much *faster* than women, the fact is that women eventually catch up until the amorous couple is functioning with the effective IQ of vinyl flooring but without the nice pattern (unless they happen to be lying on a chenille bedspread). While they are idiots, at least they are *happy* and, eventually, *contented* idiots.

But a logical question arises at this juncture—why did God create the two genders with such striking differences when it comes to sexual arousal? I mean, since the goal is to end up at the same point of romantic interest, why did God create the "slow fuse of desire" for women as opposed to the "exploding oil refinery inferno of desire" for men?

I think there are at least three key answers to this question.

First, to keep us from breeding like crazed bunnies! Can you imagine how *nuts* this world would be if women were as quickly aroused as men?

As it stands right now, if a guy pulls his wife close and whispers in her ear, "Give me one good reason I shouldn't make passionate love to you on the spot," she has sense enough to reply, "Well, we have not fully thought through the implications of having another child in the near future. Plus, we are standing in the grocery aisle."

One of the two genders needs to be able to make these close calls.

Second, men need the powerful pull of desire to overcome our natural inclination to avoid interpersonal depth. If guys were asexual, if sex were no big deal—a take-it-or-leave-it proposition—a lot of guys would be content to have guy roommates and watch tons of NASCAR racing on TV and have the relational depth of the thin layer of dust on a bookshelf.[2] We would lack that initial strong draw to those odd beings who are so very *different* from us, as evidenced by the behavior of fourth-grade boys, who typically view girls as both useless and the source of cooties.

Women have a lot of the emotive and relational qualities guys lack, qualities that in many cases we start out not knowing that we lack or not caring that we lack. But women are deeply and reflexively oriented toward deep relationships. Women positively *dive* into deep conversations about how stuff makes them *feel*.

Guys, on the other hand, may occasionally *wade* into conversations about how they feel, but those feelings are often about anger, and usually there is a BLIND referee involved. A blind, IGNORAMUS ref who deserves to be thrashed for that call! Stevie Wonder or Ray Charles could have made that call! We should legally be able to *stone that ref* for that call!

That's where guys expend their emotions when sex is not in the mix.

---

[2]Plus, the human race would be erased from the planet in one generation and the world would be taken over by cats: cats running amok, cats on all the good furniture, cats getting all the good seats at the World Series. It would not be a good world.

So God gives us this passion that is strong enough to lure us into a relationship with a much more emotional creature.

Third, God uses the female "slow burn" time to force guys to learn to communicate and grow in ways that they may otherwise miss out on. It is a cliché that women want to know what guys are really feeling deep down inside, while men want to have sex. While this is an oversimplification, there is a dose of truth in it.

Researchers say that women use roughly twice as many words per day as men (not counting all the times they tell the kids to "leave each other alone!"). So there are clearly different thresholds of desire for verbalization.

A newly married guy can come home from work, kiss his wife, hear her ask, "How was your day?" and reply, "Fine," and then want to mess around. And when he said, "Fine," he actually meant it. It might have been a perfectly fine day, but pretty unremarkable with not much to tell, so he just sums it up so they can get to the exciting stuff.

But she wants WAY more information than that.

This happened a lot with Dale and me in the early days of our marriage. I would say things were "fine" and she would get frustrated because she wanted me to explain what I had been thinking about that day.

I would get kind of defensive, because I literally did not know what she was talking about.

"I just worked. Work is work. There isn't anything to tell," I would say.

"You mean you thought about *nothing* all day? Are you saying it is even *possible* to think about *nothing* all day?" she would ask.

She might just as well have strapped me in a chair, put the bright light in my eyes, and said, "Vell, ve hass vays of makink you talk!"

As a guy who used to have male roommates, I was not used to these kinds of questions. We guys did not ask each other, "What kind of emotions did you feel today?"

We asked questions like, "Do you think we can use a blowtorch to burn that green scunge out of the refrigerator without wrecking the insulation?"

So my conversations with Dale would often end up with my declaring in exasperation, "I'm not that deep!"

"Yes, you are, you just don't know it yet!" she would reply.

And she *would not give up* drawing things out of me, asking leading questions, giving me food for thought.

Sex is what kept these early occasions from being sheer frustration and conflict. This is called leading a horse to water and making him thirsty enough to drink. I am a profoundly different person because of Dale's persistent, gentle, loving insistence that I learn to discover, and reveal, a lot of things about myself that I simply could not see at first.

Interestingly, the more a guy talks honestly with his beloved about his hopes and dreams, fears and concerns, the more amorous she becomes. So everyone wins! I don't believe this is an accident. This sounds suspiciously like something God arranged. Because He knows that, deep down, we are better, happier, and more complete people once we learn the agony and ecstasy of self-disclosure, trust, giving, and leaning on someone else. These issues are at the heart of relationship—including relationship with God himself. He will not willingly allow us to be stunted, reserved, shallow people. He is the original matchmaker, thoroughly enjoying the process of bringing a man and a woman together, and certain that if they will just listen to Him, they will be better off because of it. And He will quite happily use heavy breathing and a rapid pulse as a catalyst to get what He wants.

And what He wants is a love triangle. A man and a woman given to each other and given to the smiling God who thought the whole exquisite thing up in the first place.

Every week in church I see frail elderly couples sitting together, looking like the very picture of contentment and devotion. I am sure that in many cases, sex for them is a pleasant memory of years gone by. But the commitment, the trust, the *love* is deeper and richer and more profound than it was in those heady days of their early years as newlyweds.

And as I watch them lean on each other and hold a Bible together in unsteady hands, I realize that God got what He really wanted.

And so did they.

CHAPTER 12

All Dolled Up

Marriage allows a woman to continue engaging in a pastime she has enjoyed since childhood: dressing up her doll. Yes, gentlemen, we are all giant "Ken" figures, only with more parts.

The first big clue a guy gets that matrimony means signing away his right to choose his own clothing comes during the wedding-planning process, in which his beloved and her assorted female friends flip through catalog after catalog to find just the right "outfit" for him—an outfit that often involves something called a "cummerbund," which is nothing more than a fabric message to the world: "This guy had no choice about his attire."

But most guys figure, "What the heck. Wedding details are something women really like, so being dressed up in a shirt with frilly things down the front and a constricting band around your waist is a small price to pay for marital harmony. Besides, it's all over in an hour."

What an amusingly optimistic dunce!

Guys, there is something *prophetic* about the fact that before you begin your new life with your beloved you must first stand on a chair in a crowded tuxedo shop and model dorky black trousers while your fiancée and her mother discuss whether there is too much fabric in your crotch.

The wedding clothing decision is just the tip of the apparel iceberg. After you are married, you will notice that your wife will start offering to "help" you pick out what you should wear to go out to dinner. She will also assist you in shopping for shoes. She will start to purchase clothes for special occasions, like your birthday, Christmas, and, depending on how desperate she feels about your wardrobe, Groundhog Day, and maybe even the commemoration of National Concrete Week.

The message is twofold: (1) she wants you to look your very best, and (2) you have the clothing taste of a color-blind Philistine.

She will admit the first point, but she loves you too much to come right out and tell you that you are completely incapable of dressing yourself. Instead, she will drop subtle little hints like, "I think this blue oxford shirt looks much better on you than that *old green shirt*" or "Honey, I think the collar is getting a little frayed on that *old green shirt* you bought when President Ford was in office" or "Now, how did that *old green shirt* get caught in the garbage disposal *and* catch on fire?"

You, as a guy, may be under the impression that you are perfectly competent to dress yourself, but that is only because you are a severely fashion-impaired ignoramus, which can be proven by your shallow willingness to choose comfort over looks.

For example, your old worn-out basketball shoes, baggy shorts, and soft cotton T-shirt with the "BIG DOG" logo may be extremely comfortable, but you'll *never* see this outfit being modeled in international fashion designer competitions.

Fashion is synonymous with discomfort. Just look at women's shoes. When I was growing up, I would watch in fascination as my mother hobbled unsteadily toward the car on Sunday mornings just so she could be fashionable and wear high heels to church. These shoes were pointed at the toe like a paper airplane, and the heel consisted of a four-inch-high, one-quarter-inch-wide spike. They were more like stilts than shoes. If a completely demented cobbler set out to invent the most torturous, ridiculous footwear he could imagine, he could not have done any better than my mom's church shoes.

The split second we got home every week my mom would whip those babies off her feet and sit on the couch, rubbing her ankles and moaning.

"Why do you wear them if they hurt so much?" I would ask.

"I want to look nice," she would say with a grimace. "Now be a nice boy and get me an Ace bandage and some aspirin."

Women are not content to suffer the slings and arrows of outrageous fashion alone, however, which is why they invented the tie. I have not done any research on the tie, but I know it could not have been invented by a guy, for much the same reason I can confidently state that booster shots were not invented by a toddler. There is no way we would voluntarily impose this kind of suffering on ourselves. A tie is sort of like an Old West hanging but without the trial and the last meal.

Because I have to dress nicely for work anyway ("nicely" being defined as a pressed shirt, a tie, slacks, and those dorky wing-tip shoes that every professional male has been forced to wear since Ohio was admitted to the Union), I do not terribly mind that my wife assists me in my wardrobe decisions. I'll admit that, without her input, I do tend to wear shirts that don't quite match my pants, ties that don't quite match my shirts, and socks that don't quite match each other because I accidentally grabbed a blue one and a gray one.

So we don't really disagree all that much about looking "nice for work" or "nice for church" or "nice for dinner." The real conflict arises when I get home from work or church or a dinner date and I rip off my "nice" clothes and throw on what Dale refers to simply as *"those"* (as in, "you aren't going to wear *those*, are you?").

"Those" is said with a tone that is one part disgust, one part dread, and one part incredulity.

In my case, "those" currently consists of extremely worn and baggy sweat pants, tennis shoes dating back to the Mayflower Compact, and a hugely oversized blue T-shirt containing as much fabric as a formal dining room tablecloth. These are the most comfortable clothes I own, and I would gladly pay five times their original purchase price if I could find another complete set in exactly the same condition. Because I WANT TO BE COMFORT-ABLE when I finally get home or have a day off!

So I wear "those" clothes at every possible opportunity, even though Dale cringes and shudders when I walk into the room.

How did we ever get to the point where uncomfortable

and often stupid-looking clothes became synonymous with "nice"?

I have a theory. Have you ever noticed how royalty, especially of some time past, wore absurdly nonfunctional clothing, often employing yards and yards of fabric, huge feathers, and jewelry heavy enough to sink a Coast Guard patrol boat? They could barely move in those clothes, much less clip the royal shrubbery or dig the royal moat or lube the royal carriage. But I think that was exactly the point. I think those fancy clothes were designed, in part, to underscore the message, "We are royalty, and, unlike you underlings, we do not do labor. Ha, ha, ha, ha!"

The problem is that no matter how stupid royalty looked, and despite the fact that it took royalty the better part of an hour to simply get undressed enough to use the royal urinal, the next tier of "wannabe" royalty (your dukes, duchesses, and trial lawyers) tried to dress a lot like the king and queen so as to be "in."

This even filtered down to the "professional class" of the time, all of whom dressed as "nicely" as possible while still holding down jobs, which means they were trying to work while wearing clothes that were specifically designed to make work nearly impossible. Thus, the manual laborers got all the comfortable, functional clothes and merchants got stuck with thin blue stretchy socks with little diamond patterns embroidered on them (which, by the way, are still being sold in the men's department of Sears).

It is thus with some envy that corporate executives look out their high-rise offices at the window washers on the other side of the glass who get to wear loose-fitting overalls and white cushioned socks.

And it is with a twinge of irony that I read in the book

of James, "Suppose a man comes into your meeting wearing a gold ring and fine clothes, and a poor man in shabby clothes also comes in. If you show special attention to the man wearing fine clothes . . . have you not discriminated among yourselves and become judges with evil thoughts?" (2:2–9).

I'm certainly guilty of envy, but I'm envying the custodian who was vacuuming the Sunday school rooms Saturday night wearing sweats and a T-shirt and whistling while he worked.

As a Christian, I believe that Jesus, although He looked like us, was actually God visiting the earth. And it has not escaped my notice that when God showed up on the planet, He did not dress like royalty. He did not wear burgundy Florsheim wing-tip shoes, and He certainly never wore a tie.

No, God wore the normal, functional, comfortable clothes of the everyday people.

Does anyone besides me see a message here?

I wonder if the Sears men's department would special-order a toga?

CHAPTER 13

The Path Is Narrow (and So Is the Field)

Some people, particularly (but not exclusively) people who still have acne and have only been driving for a short period of time, reason that as long as they don't get pregnant it is OK for them to have sex with someone they are not married to. If God even enters into their thinking about this subject, they ask themselves questions like, "Why would God create me with this powerful desire if He didn't want me to express it? Either it is OK to express my sexuality or God is a sadistic killjoy."

However, there is a third possibility that they have either failed to consider or refused to accept, and that is: He *does* want them to have sex—just not yet. Even if they could be absolutely sure they would not get pregnant, God has His reasons for telling them to wait. And when it comes to this subject (and any *other* subject, for that matter), God has both the right and the wisdom to call the shots.

And He is both emphatic and unambiguous in calling the shots on this subject: **no marriage, no sex**. He is perfectly delighted to bless our lovemaking as long as we make a lifelong commitment first.

Not "think about making a commitment while we live together."

Not "make a commitment when we can afford it."

And not "eventually commit to someone after I have played the field."

With God there is no "field" to "play." You get to have a *single blade of grass* from the field, and you stick with *that* blade of grass until one of you DIES. You can look the field over (as long as the field is dressed decently) prior to picking your special blade of grass. And you can date several of them while you are considering which one to pick. But you only get one blade of grass out of the entire field.

When confronted with these constraints, there are people who will reply that if this is actually God's point of view, it is an extremely *narrow* and *restrictive* one.

Well, *duh!*

Of course it is! Two-way traffic lanes are also restrictive and narrow, and if you decide to wander over the line you could find yourself plowing head on into a five-ton Mack truck loaded down with asparagus, which would put a real damper on your love life, now wouldn't it? Sometimes "narrow and restrictive" is good news, not bad.

And when it comes to the issue of potential sexual partners, God couldn't have narrowed the field down any more if He wanted to. Of all the billions of people in the world, He says you can pick *just one* to have and to hold till death do you part.

But this is not cruelty. Cruelty would be to give us our immense emotional and biological needs and then say, "Thou shalt never consummate your desire under *any* circumstances, even if you fall in love and make a lifelong commitment! *Bwah, ha, ha, ha, ha!*" while scary pipe organ music plays in the background.

But that is not what He has done.

He has defined the parameters of what is healthy and good and holy and ultimately the most fulfilling of human relationships. Although the formal wedding vows—"for better or for worse, for richer, for poorer, in sickness and in health, till death do you part"—were not specifically stated by God, they are concepts extracted directly from His Word.

Indeed, He positively *rails* against the evil of abandoning one's marriage and family.

"I hate divorce!" He thunders from the Old Testament.

"Husbands, love your wives, just as Christ loved the church and gave himself up for her," He decrees in the New Testament, going on to point out that Jesus bled and died all for the sake of a permanent relationship with us. God is *into* commitment.

So let's be very clear that God is not asking, or suggesting, or advising. He is *demanding* that we make the "mother of all commitments" before we make love, and He is *demanding* that we stay in it for the long haul once we say, "I do." Loyalty, sacrifice, and love to the very end are core issues to Him.

And He is only requiring from us a small measure of what He requires of himself. In ways we cannot ever fully understand, God himself went through hell for us for the sake of love. Jesus is the model of what God thinks about commitment. He held back nothing for our sake. Our entrance into heaven came at the great cost of His life.

Think of the soldier who died battling the Nazis so his wife and kids could live in freedom, and multiply that passion and devotion by a factor of several billion. That will give you an idea of what motivated God to secure heaven for us. That is the kind of God we are dealing with.

So it is not at all surprising that it matters very much to Him that we who are made in His image also learn to practice commitment, loyalty, sacrifice, and love to the very end.

Having laid out God's position on this issue as I understand it, I have to acknowledge that there are extraordinary extenuating circumstances that sometimes make the aforementioned kind of commitment virtually impossible. God understands this—with great sorrow. He recognizes the horrific damage that is done when one partner breaks the marriage vows (which is why He says "THOU SHALT NOT!"), but if that happens, He appears to leave the option open to the injured spouse to salvage the relationship or to step away from it.

And, of course, He does not want anyone hanging around to get beat up or to endanger herself or her children in any way. You know the kinds of serious situations I am talking about.

But most troubled marriages are not in those kinds of extreme circumstances. Rather, there may be some stress, some hurt, some bad communication, some toying with the idea of cheating or leaving. And I am simply pointing out that if married partners will employ the kind of giving and sacrifice and selfless love that God intends, and if we will lean on Him and lean on good people who will cheer us on and help us succeed, our marriages will never get to the point of desperation and destruction.

I know I am getting heavier here than I usually do, but I have HAD IT with seeing marriages and families I know and love blown to smithereens because of selfishness.

I have known Andy* since I was in high school. I was present at his wedding when he promised God and everyone else that he would give himself completely to Anne, forsaking all others, until death should part them.

He lied. I don't believe that he intended to lie. But I don't really care about his intentions. The fact remains that he chose to break his vows, which means he chose to become a liar, a cheat, and an adulterer.

And then he blamed Anne for his lies! If she were only better, he wouldn't have had to go looking for a bimbo to "bond" with.

So he is also a *cruel* liar.

Anne is not perfect. Is anyone? But she loved Andy and stood with him through all the ups and downs of their lives. She is a truly beautiful person. She gave birth to their really great kids, and in general she is the kind of woman any rational man would want. But Andy decided to flirt—to look around. He wanted something more.

It didn't matter that he was taking the emotional equivalent of a machine gun to Anne and the kids by doing so. Oh sure, he *claimed* he still cared about them. He told the kids he still loved them, *but* . . .

They were bright enough to get the point that *"but"* meant he didn't love them enough to come home and be

---

*Names have been changed.

their daddy. Children are not fools. They know that you are what you *do*, not what you *say*.

I know that God was hammering away at Andy's heart during this ordeal, trying to get him to repent. But we are free beings, and that means we are equally free to be loving partners or selfish jerks. Andy chose to be a selfish jerk.

Do I sound harsh? Judgmental? I'm pulling punches compared to what God says.

Take a look at what the Scripture pronounces when discussing people who engage in flagrant sin with no hint of remorse: "If ye endure chastening, God dealeth with you as with sons; for what son is he whom the father chasteneth not? But if ye be without chastisement, whereof all are partakers, then are ye bastards, and not sons" (Hebrews 12:7–8 KJV).

Andy never came back home. Last time I heard, he was living with his new girlfriend. He'll probably dump her someday. That's what the statistics say. Then he'll probably find yet another woman and start the wretched process all over again.

Some marriage books laud "affairs" as experiences that actually add to a good marriage. These authors think a range of sexual partners is healthy and meaningful and beneficial. These authors are all idiots. And the people who believe them are idiots too or at best self-deceived.

A wake of emotional destruction follows in the path of people who decide to forsake their vows, much like when a tornado plows through a neighborhood. There is wreckage everywhere, stunned and bewildered people, memories torn to shreds and spread like trash all over the countryside. Where there are kids involved, they pay a particularly brutal price. So it is no big surprise that God says divorce is something He *hates*.

But the adults who once swore before God and the assembled witnesses that they would be there for each other, even when life got hard, also pay a price. Even God pays a price, because our actions cause Him grief.

So what do you do if you have already blown it?

For starters, admit the truth to yourself, to God, and to the people you have hurt. If possible, make things as right as you can. Contact a minister (the kind who respects the Scriptures) and seek professional guidance.

And if you are in a new marriage, a prior marriage having been torpedoed, then do everything in your power to make *this* one work. Don't let it happen again if you have any control whatsoever (and you probably do).

I don't mean to leave anyone in despair, but I do not want to dance around a subject that I think is critically important. Besides, as you can tell, the issue hits close to home. I have friends who, as I write this, are deciding whether or not they are willing to stay together. I want to scream.

I am a humor writer, and I try to make most of my points through that medium. But some things just don't have a funny angle to them.

So, having laid out all this heavy stuff, let me also affirm that God is the God of the second chance. Even people who have badly blown their marriage are not relegated by God to the "damaged goods" section.

King David was the greatest king Israel had ever seen. David truly loved God, and God truly loved David. But one day, in a moment of self-inflicted weakness, David cheated on his wife, got another woman pregnant, and subsequently even ordered the assassination of the other woman's husband in a desperate attempt to keep the lid on the whole wicked mess.

David was eventually confronted by a man of God sent for the very purpose of revealing this awful series of sins but who also gave David the opportunity to repent. David did repent, in wrenching agony and bitter tears.

God forgave him. God will always forgive a man or a woman who honestly turns from his or her sin and seeks God's face. That is the whole point of the death and resurrection of Jesus. The cross allows God the freedom to forgive the otherwise unforgivable.

But forgiven though he was, David and his family paid a terrible price for his adultery and accompanying sins. His kids also had serious moral failures. I wonder if they would have turned out differently had he not set such a horrible example.

You reap what you sow. That is right out of the Bible. If you are even toying with breaking your wedding vows, and nothing I have said so far has changed your mind, then I would caution you that you are messing with a God who takes cheating very, very, very seriously. Don't cross Him on this.

I won't take this dark chapter any further. I am not a professional marriage counselor. I am just an imperfect guy who is married to the almost perfect woman of my dreams. I don't have the expertise to offer counsel about specific circumstances. There are real marriage books out on the market that do.

But I do know the end result God is after, because it is written in glaringly large type all over the Bible. It is best summed up in the words of Jesus shortly before He allowed Roman guards to nail Him to a cross in order to pay for our sins—including the sins of infidelity and hurting our kids: "Love one another, just as I have loved you."

CHAPTER 14

The Car of My Schemes

It was the kind of car most guys only dream about—a painstakingly restored 1957 Chevy Bel Air with an off-white top, a deep burgundy body, and crushed velvet interior—and it had been delivered to *my* driveway earlier that day.

"It *is* beautiful," my wife agreed. "But not very practical."

"Practical, schmacktical!" I retorted, employing powerful logic to overcome her objection. "This is the quintessential American car! In Detroit people can legally *marry* this car! We'll just take a few commonsense precautions, like parking it in the garage at night, putting a cover on it in public parking lots, and hiring 'Vinnie the Enforcer' to follow it wherever it goes."

There was NO way we were getting rid of that car.

"There's one other thing," Dale said. "Mark just turned sixteen, which means he is going to be wanting to drive a *lot*, and I can just envision an absolute whining festival over who gets the keys. I don't think I can take all the sniveling and begging."

I smiled and nodded in the condescending "there, there" manner Dale has always found so endearing.

"I mean it," she warned. "Look me in the eyes and read just how serious I am. I do *not* want this car to turn into a source of conflict. You are going to have to be really tough."

"It won't be a problem," I assured her.

Fifteen minutes later . . .

"Oh, please, please, please, please, *puh-leeeeeeease?* I promise I'll stick to back roads! It won't get a scratch. I won't eat while I drive! I just want to show it off to my friends! Please? C'mon! Please?"

Dale stormed into the room in the middle of the beg-a-thon.

"Is this about what I *think* it is about?" she demanded.

Mark cast a desperate, pleading look at her.

"Mom, Dad is whining about my car again! I thought you had a talk with him."

"Oh, pleeeeeeeeeeeeeeeeease," I said again, falling to my knees and clutching his ankles. "Just let me take it around the block!"

"I told you already! You need to show some maturity first!" Mark replied firmly.

"Oh, *that's* a good one," Dale said dryly.

"But I didn't mean to rev the engine at the traffic light," I whimpered. "The gas pedal got stuck! It wasn't my fault that the guy next to us thought I wanted to race!"

Dale's jaw tightened as she looked at me.

"Tell me, was it the 'no sniveling' or the 'no begging' part that was confusing?" she asked in that slow, measured tone that means the addressee should forward himself to another room.

It just wasn't fair!

My father had called me a week earlier to explain that he wanted Mark to have the '57, which had been in the Meurer family for more than two decades.

"Why can't you give it to ME?" I wailed. "I'm your own flesh and blood SON! Mark is a distant relative at best—a virtual STRANGER! In fact, I have always suspected he was accidentally switched with another baby at the hospital. Don't compound the tragedy by signing the '57 over to this shameless IMPOSTOR."

"It isn't a gift, son. I am going to let my *grandson* buy it from me," Dad explained. "He needs a good deal on some wheels now that he is sixteen. Besides, I think it will help him mature. It will teach him responsibility."

"But I need to mature, too! And I still need to learn responsibility! Just ask Dale," I cried.

"I think it is too late for you," Dad said. "But I still have hope for your kids."

This horrible situation was made all the more horrible by the fact that all my life I have had a series of ugly, loser cars that broke down at every opportunity and made no secret of the fact that they hated me. I have owned a 1969 Volkswagen hatchback, which is *not* to be confused with those charming little VW bugs we all know and love. No, the hatchback would have been better named the "hunchback." Pedestrians would literally clutch their ears and start yelling, "The bells!!! The bells!!!" when I drove by.

Then I had a 1977 AMC Pacer, which was voted "Ugliest Car of the Year" by *Motor Trend* magazine. The Pacer looked like you took a Ford Pinto and *inflated* it until the windows bulged out like toad eyes.

I had other even WORSE cars, which I am so embarrassed about that I will not even mention them other than to note that when someone crashed into one of them and totaled it, Dale began jumping up and down singing, "Ding-Dong! The Witch Is Dead!"

I *deserved* to finally drive a cool car to make up for all my prior humiliation!

I tried negotiating a deal with Mark, but he was a brutally tough bargainer.

"Mark, I'll paint flames on the sides of the station wagon; think how much more storage space you'll have than in the Chevy! It will be a straight-across trade. You don't have to give me a dime, and I'll even throw in one of those air fresheners that look like a little cardboard pine tree."

"How tempting," he mused. "Maybe you could also offer to let me walk on hot coals or fling myself off the dam."

"Sure! It would be sort of like a big waterslide! And it would probably feel refreshing after those coals!" I replied.

Needless to say, I am still driving my aged wagon, and Mark has one of the coolest cars in town.

To add insult to injury, Dale won't even ride with me in the station wagon since I had those flames painted on the fenders.

Oh well. God is probably just using this situation to teach me lessons like being content with what I have and rejoicing in someone else's good fortune.

Oh, and let's not forget humility. I am learning a *real* good lesson in that.

CHAPTER 15

Out of This World

I was scanning the newspaper when Brad asked a question that had been plagueing him for at least fifteen minutes.

"If humans abducted an alien, would it still be called an 'alien abduction'?"

There are two broad categories of discussion you can have with your children while you are holding a newspaper: (1) the kind where you can mumble an answer and continue to read, and (2) the kind where you kiss off the fifty cents you invested because it will be "olds" by the time you get back to it. The category is determined by whether your child accepts whatever monosyllable you mumble for an answer as you attempt to continue to read.

"Yes," I mumbled.

Pause.

"So how come whether an alien abducts us or we abduct an alien, it is still called an 'alien abduction'?" he continued.

"Then, no," I replied, flipping the page.

Pause.

"So if an alien abducts us, would it be called a 'human abduction'?"

There is no persistence like the persistence of a ten-year-old boy.

"Yes," I muttered, poring over the presidential "scandal *du jour*."

Pause.

"So if it is a 'human abduction' when an alien abducts a human, what do you call it when a human abducts another human?"

"Kidnapping," I sighed.

Pause.

"Can you be *kidnapped* by an alien, or just *abducted* by an alien?" he asked.

"Ask Mom."

"OK."

I went back to reading the paper. Soon, however, I had a growing sense that I was being, well, *observed*. Like eyes were boring into the back of my head. I tried to shake it off, but it grew. And grew. And grew! It felt like some kind of unearthly force field had me in its grip!

I whirled around and was shocked to find stern, unblinking, spooky eyes staring at me. I had seen those eyes before! It was back when . . . when . . . I went with my wife to the fabric store and got kind of bored after about thirty seconds and began making droll comments about not being able to take much more of this excitement, and my wife looked up from a bolt of periwinkle and I felt my will to live being sucked right out of my body.

It was that stare again. Dale was unamused.

"Dave, you were *completely* ignoring Brad. It was *rude*. Who else would you treat that way? And someday you are going to really miss these times when he was willing and eager to ask you questions," she said.

Gulp.

Guilt.

"I think we need to treat our boys with the same common courtesy we would show our friends and each other," she continued. "After all, *I* would be offended if you kept reading the paper while *I* was talking with you."

"You're right. I'm sorry," I said to Dale. "I'll make it a point to apologize to Brad as soon as—"

My voice trailed off as my eyes were pulled back down to the page.

The paper was ripped from my hands and is probably still circling Jupiter. The Mother Ship was about to open fire with its deadly blast rays, but the rebel force launched itself from the couch and made the jump to light speed.

I have always had a problem with tuning people out when I am reading. I think I picked it up from my father, who had the same flaw. We kids would even make a game out of asking preposterous things of my dad while he was reading, because we knew he was on autopilot.

"Dad," I would say as he buried his nose in the *Daily News*.

"Mmmm," he would reply.

"I need you to double my allowance, give me your car, and send me to Tahiti with your credit card."

"OK," he would reply, flipping the page.

Then it was my brother Jim's turn.

"Dad, we have an audience with Queen Elizabeth in fifteen minutes. The Royal Family is going to cook tacos for us and then take us skydiving. We won it in a raffle. But you have to put on a powdered wig before the press gets here."

"Ask your mother," he would mumble.

(Jim won that round.)

So you can't pin all the blame on me for my rude newspaper passion. Some of this is genetic.

Nevertheless, one of the truly great things God does through our spouses is to help us see, and work to overcome, our little blind spots. Or, in some cases, our blind *acreage*. Because at one point in my life, in addition to newspapers, I was *also* glued to obscure political journals, the television news, the talking head shows on Public Television, and raucous congressional fights on C-SPAN. I would be completely oblivious to my kids, my wife, the friends we invited over for dinner, and the fire fighters who were screaming at me to "jump!" because the house was ablaze.

I did not realize how obnoxious and obsessed I was being. When you are single, you can develop all kinds of self-centered behaviors that may not really matter all that much if the only company you have is a dog or even a roommate. Before I had a wife and family, I could easily read a novel for nine hours at a time. This activity is morally benign in and of itself. But your use of time takes on a new dimension when other people are involved (so does your use of the milk carton, which no longer substitutes for a personal drinking glass, as Dale made *emphatically* clear the first time she saw me swigging from a gallon container).

And killing a few hours in front of the TV can be OK in one context but not in another—such as when you have been working and going to school for seventy-five hours each week and your family needs to interact with you on a deeper level than what can occur between station breaks.

Ultimately, I pulled the plug on myself for the sake of my family. I canceled the newspaper and sharply restricted my intake of TV so I could focus on my family. I learned to moderate my obsession with politics.*

The Bible notes that God sometimes speaks in a "still, small voice." When He needs to crank up the volume, He often uses our spouse. Odds are, God will not personally stand in front of you, snatch the newspaper you are engrossed in, and say, "Your children need you to play with them. You can read that later."

But even though He did not personally deliver the message, I think it was precisely the message He wanted me to hear.

My wife is God's main way of helping me learn to really listen.

For instance, I thought Brad's "alien inquisition" was just a bunch of standard kid-type questions about semantics (albeit rather *odd* standard kid-type questions about semantics). Dale, who listens on a deeper level, was concerned that Brad was really getting into this alien thing. He, as well as scores of other fifth graders, had been reading a lot of suspenseful short stories about alien abductions. Some of the kids began to sort of believe it. For

---

*Interestingly, within a couple of years I was offered a job—out of the blue—as a congressional aide, where as part of my daily routine I would scan a "morning digest" of all the big news and leave the TV tuned to congressional debates while I went about my work. So I was getting *paid* to do stuff I wanted to do anyway, and it didn't intrude into family time. Sometimes when you give something up, you get it back in a better way.

some, it was crossing the line from fantasy to faith.

I decided the best response was to go low-key.

We were eating dinner when I said to Mark and Brad, "You know, I was just thinking about how huge the universe is. Astronomers say it is billions of light-years across. There are entire solar systems we don't even know about. It kind of makes you wonder what's out there."

I instantly had their attention.

"I was thinking, with all that space and all those galaxies, somewhere on one of those planets, far from our telescopes, there just *has* to be a really good Mexican restaurant."

The boys stared at me with arched eyebrows, then looked at each other.

"That has *got* to be the most lame thing I have ever heard," Brad said.

"Think about it," I chided. "Planets, space, light years, *burritos*—see how they just kind of flow? Kinda makes you wonder, huh?"

Brad started to laugh.

Mark just rolled his eyes, refusing to dignify my comments with a rebuttal.

"Just a thought," I said, shrugging.

But aliens quietly reverted to the stuff of stories and movies—until Mark came home one day from church youth group and commented, "Hey! The Bible says there are aliens!"

"What?!?" exclaimed Brad.

"It says WE are 'strangers and *aliens*' on the earth!" continued Mark.

"*Cooooooooooool!*" replied Brad.

Sometimes when you give something up, you get it back in a better way.

CHAPTER 16

The Affair

My affair began, as I presume so many of them do, as an innocent enough "Let's have dinner after this big project is over" sort of thing. We decided on a restaurant called Karen's. Nice but informal. A relaxing atmosphere after a grueling midterm exam at the university.

I was coming down off a stress-induced buzz. The conversation was sparkling and enjoyable, so we allowed it to continue long after the apple pie was gone and the coffee cups were empty.

I had always fancied myself a rather ordinary family man. I had a wife, two kids, a mortgage, and unfinished household projects. My normal routine was to drive the relatively straight and narrow one-hour commute home after my last class at 4:45 P.M., play with my young boys, eat dinner, hit the books, chat with my wife a bit, hit the sack, go to work the next morning and do it all over again.

A measured routine. An efficient way to balance school, work, and family.

A dull and predictable rut.

And it was wearing me down.

Dangerously so.

I knew I needed a break, but I tried to just keep gutting it out day by day.

I occasionally found myself envying, even resenting, the other students I saw strolling into The Bear for an evening of frivolity and heaven only knows what else as I trudged my well-worn path homeward.

But there was something so deliciously different, so fresh and exhilarating about this dinner out with good company that I found myself resisting the idea of going home too soon. She was obviously in no hurry to leave either. We were having such a mutually great time.

We decided to go for a leisurely drive. Just to talk. But one thing led to another, and the particulars are private, thank you. Suffice it to say that we found a spot for more than just a talk, a million miles away from my hometown, and homework, and unfinished household projects.

"Do you want to have an affair?" she asked.

"Yes," I replied, taken aback by the bluntness of the question, but flattered and excited by the thought. And thus it began.

We made the plans that inevitably accompany a hushed relationship: adjusting our schedules, agreeing on places, crafting alibis.

When I had made the promise six years previously to love, honor, and cherish, I had never dreamed that marriage, even passion, could become old hat. No newlywed can fathom that it can somehow become old. But it can, and it does, especially if you are unaware that marriage is not a perpetual-motion machine. It is a delicate plant, and without constant attention it begins to wither under the heat of everyday life.

An affair becomes possible, and perhaps even probable, when the first flame has dimmed through neglect. The exciting alternative seems to outweigh the original relationship, the risk of being caught, and the guilt that accompanies betrayal.

And an affair is nothing if it is not betrayal, which is why guilt always accompanies the furtive fling. Justifying the affair therefore becomes crucial, lest the guilt completely destroy you. So all affairs are exercises in not only the deception of another but also the attempt to deceive oneself as well. I know several guys who have been there.

But in my particular case, guilt and self-deception were not issues, because it was my *wife* who asked me to have an affair with her that day after dinner at Karen's. My sweet, insightful, ever-romantic Dale found the secret to a thrilling, exotic, guilt-free "affair"—to go sneaking around with the person you married in the first place.

CHAPTER 17

The Regrettable Sculpture Incident

"I want you to draw the soul of a tree," announced Mr. Widlund, my seventh-grade art teacher. "It is due at the end of the period. You may begin now."

And I thought it was hard to diagram a *sentence* in English class! This assignment was *absurd!*

I raised my hand.

"Trees don't have souls," I explained, thinking that if I perhaps clarified this obvious point we could try the bowl of fruit again.

"Use your imagination," he replied.

I hated it when he said stuff like that. Art was not about imagination, art was about copying something real as closely as possible. I liked paintings by Norman Rockwell. Mr. Widlund liked paintings by weird foreigners who drew melting clocks drooping off tables. Artwise, we were the Hatfields and the McCoys.

But I had him this time.

"Sister Mary Marie told our catechism class that only humans have souls. The pope is on her side. So this assignment would violate my core beliefs. I must therefore be a conscientious objector," I said.

I knew that a mere art teacher was no match for Sister Mary Marie and the pope. He would probably have to excuse me from the class and let me have an Orange Crush in the teachers' lounge.

"Then draw what you think the soul of a tree would look like if trees had souls," he replied.

Ohhhh. This guy was smooooth.

"Class," he said, clapping his hands for attention. "There is no right or wrong on this assignment. This is about emotion, feeling, expression. Just draw. Just flow with it. Feel the tree. Express the tree. *BE* the tree."

You gotta bear in mind that this was the 1970s.

So I got to work with the rest of my classmates, and forty-seven minutes later I stood in line to hand in my work and leave.

"Provocative," Mr. Widlund said to the kid three places in front of me.

"Very emotive. I see a lot of passion here," he said to the next one.

"Oh. A lot of regret in this tree. Very good," he said to the next.

He glanced at my submission, winced, and handed it back.

"*That* is not the soul of a tree," he said.

"You said there is no right or wrong on this!" I retorted.

"You have successfully created an exception," he said.

"WHY?!?"

"You drew a *tree*, David," he said. "That was not the assignment."

"But I think the soul of a tree would look like a tree!"

"Use your imagination. You have ninety seconds until the bell rings. Give me the soul of a tree within one minute. And use some emotion," he called after me as I stormed back to my desk.

I was livid.

I grabbed a brown colored pencil, drew sharp scribbles and circles on a white piece of paper, walked to the front of the class, and thrust it at Mr. Widlund.

"Harsh," he observed.

"It was an angry tree," I said.

He gave me an A.

While up until that point I had merely not understood modern art, I now became obsessed with a mission to expose it.

"It's a total scam," I complained later that day to my parents. "All you have to do is scribble or throw paint at paper and claim it represents 'the soul of a maple' or 'the suffering of the moon' or 'the enraged carburetor off a 1962 Studebaker' and you can get an A and even have imbeciles PAY you for it at stupid galleries in San Francisco."

They just laughed, but I was seriously incensed.

So you can imagine how hard I had to bite my tongue when the person I married just so happened to not only appreciate modern art but also create it.

I stared at the complex pieces of Z-shaped black and green acrylic she placed on the table and tried to think of something complimentary to say. She had spent untold hours forming, bending, sanding, and manipulating this . . . this . . . stuff.

"What is it?" I asked.

"What do you mean, 'what is it'?" Dale replied.

Oops.

"What is it supposed to be?" I asked.

"It isn't supposed to *be* anything. It's just a study of line and form."

This was not going well.

"Oh. Well, now that you mention it, that's exactly what it looks like."

"That statement makes no sense whatsoever. You need to learn to appreciate a wider range of art," she said.

I was doomed to have my horizons expanded.

She brought out an art book and we looked at pages and pages of sculptures, paintings, huge metal things in front of buildings, and assorted other stuff that individuals or government entities had absolutely paid through the nose for—and none of it looked *anything* like a bowl of fruit.

We went to art shows.

We went to museums.

We went to art galleries.

She would gaze at a river scene by Claude Monet and get tears in her eyes.

I would get a headache.

"He must have had a terrible vision problem; all his paintings are so fuzzy," I commented, squinting at the canvas.

"He was an *impressionist!*" Dale replied.

"He did impressions, too? Was that because no one bought his fuzzy paintings?"

She shook her head but did not give up on me.

One day she brought out a cardboard box containing a sculpture she had spent a few weeks on while in college. It was a sleek assortment of curved pieces of wood rising from a highly polished black acrylic base and topped with a combination of buffed aluminum and green Plexiglas.

"What do you think of it?" she asked.

I had already learned "What is it?" is not the correct response.

"Um, it looks like a study of line and form," I replied nervously.

"Actually, I meant this as a representation of photo-tropism," she said. "The arching wood represents the power of nature as the plant twists and climbs toward the sun, the touch of metal at the top represents the minerals in the soil, and the green represents the life in the plant."

"Oh," I replied in much the same way a deer looking into your headlights would reply "Oh" if he were capable of making vowel sounds.

"Do you think this would look good on our coffee table?" she asked.

I was suddenly back in seventh grade standing at the desk of Mr. Widlund. All my pent-up antagonism about hoity-toity, brie-on-crackers, fancy-schmancy, over-my-head art rose to the surface in an inartistic belch of emotion.

"But it doesn't *look* like *anything!*" I blurted out.

I still refer to this event as "the regrettable sculpture incident."

I immediately regretted the outburst, but you can't suck words back into your mouth like my dad did with smoke rings.

Dale quietly began packing the sculpture back into the box.

I felt like the stupid cretin that I was.

"I'm sorry."

"That's OK. We don't have to have it out if you don't like it."

I wish she would have unloaded on me. Anything but quietly wrap it in old newspaper and put it away. I offered muted protest, but what could I say? My stupid words were still lying on the table, crowding out any space for her sculpture.

My wife is one of those souls who values honesty more than she values someone trying to make her feel good by saying something they don't really believe. Therefore, she actually was not crushed by my incredibly stupid and rude reaction, which is the only way I can now honestly characterize my comments.

I was a moron. A barbarian. A dolt.

But she did not hold it against me. She recognized that it was the spontaneous reaction of an art putz. And she quietly decided to *still* not give up on me.

We went to plays.

We went to concerts.

We visited traveling exhibits—carved jade from ancient China, winter scenes by the French impressionists, the charcoal sketches of Leonardo da Vinci. This was all stuff I probably never would have done had I not married an artist.

There is no aisle you can walk down to convert from an art doofus to an art appreciator. It isn't a quick event, like a birth. It is more like building a brick wall or, in my case, building the Great Wall of China. But Dale kept building and building and building.

Years later Dale was reading to me from the collected works of G. K. Chesterton, one of her favorite poets and writers. Chesterton was contrasting the differences between art from the Buddhist and Christian perspectives. The Asian art emphasized the closed-eyed, introspective individual disconnected from all others. The Christian art tended to show figures looking out toward others or up toward God—it was relational. These different approaches to art substantially captured the different worldviews of these two very different faiths.

The introspective, individual quest for "enlightenment" contrasted with the "God and others" approach we see in Christianity.

A light clicked on, and for the first time I really understood that art is an unwritten, nonverbal form of communication. I now see that the message of much modern art is, "I don't have any talent and I hope you are idiot enough to pay me for this stuff, because if you asked me to draw a bowl of fruit you might just as well ask me to pole-vault across Nevada."

But *other* modern art is saying, "There is a wonderful order in this world God has made" or "Your wife has way more imagination and artistic talent than you do, and she even understands words like 'phototropism,' and you should count your blessings that God has allowed you to have her in your life so you can grow beyond your former cretin self."

That's quite a bit of nonverbal communication to pack into a simple sculpture.

As for Dale's sculpture, it now stands proudly on a

shelf in my office for all the world to see. When people ask me what it means, I say it represents an art cretin rising out of his prejudice and toward an appreciation of his artistic wife.

CHAPTER 18

To Shop or Not to Shop

My wife really appreciates it when I go with her to stores and help her pick out the clothes she is not going to buy. She also likes me to accompany her to the mall to look at the draperies she is not going to purchase, the shoes she is not going to get, and the household furnishings she is going to decide against.

She calls this "shopping."

To me, the term "shopping" conjures up an image of money being exchanged for merchandise. I view shopping as an act of commerce, a simple economic transaction, something to just get out of the way and be done with so you can get on to whatever is next on the list of things to get done.

To Dale, "shopping" is more like "courting." There are no hasty decisions to be made. The object under consideration needs to be visited again and again over long periods of time, sometimes years, prior to saying, "I do." *Purchase in haste, repent at leisure* is Dale's motto—with "haste" being defined as "sometime this decade."

It would be unfair of me to pounce on this contrast and make sweeping generalizations about how men and women approach shopping, so I will merely note that ALL women are like this and ALL men can't stand it, which is why we guys whimper and try to hide when our wives ask us to go shopping because we know they are really asking us to go "not shopping."

Women view the act of not shopping as a form of recreation, or education, or entertainment. Men view it as the nonproductive use of time, or sheer boredom, or the complete loss of precious moments of our life that we can *never* regain, as if life isn't short enough already, and for crying out loud if she likes the blue shoes why doesn't she just BUY them so we can get out of here before the next ice age starts and . . . "They look GREAT on you! Can we go now?"

Our greatly divergent opinions about both the joys and the wisdom of shopping without spending money were creating tension in our relationship, and I realized I was going to have to broach this subject with Dale. I needed to approach it cautiously because I did not want to convey the message that I did not want to spend time with her. I did want to spend time with her, very much so, but my eyes were glazing over as we walked hand-in-hand, peering in windows and ducking into various stores. Fabric stores were the absolute worst; clerks regularly had to call in the paramedics because I would slip into a coma once we hit the seersucker aisle.

Summoning all of my diplomatic skills, I approached Dale and said, "Honey, I love you more than I know how to say, but if you ever ask me to enter the House of Fabrics again I will hurl myself off a cliff."

Dale immediately sensed that I had reached my shopping limit. This is an example of that uncanny "woman's intuition" you hear so much about.

Marriage calls for a lot of compromise. This is a live-or-die word that you need to learn if you are going to succeed in matrimony. Rather than pout or get her feelings hurt, Dale worked with me to identify the stores that I really despised, the stores I could tolerate, and the stores that were actually OK as long as we had some kind of time limit associated with it (sometimes measured in nano-seconds). We also found that while I would prefer to be court-martialed and shot before I would enter a craft store, I actually enjoyed going into gardening and "outdoor" kinds of shops. So when she wants to go to one of the "awful" stores, she goes alone or takes a friend.

This spirit of compromise worked for quite a few months, until one evening when we were driving by an automotive dealership and I was preparing to pull into the lot, Dale said, "I don't think I quite feel up to looking at cars again."

"What do you mean 'again'?" I retorted. "We haven't been to a car lot since Tuesday!"

"I know, but I don't feel up to it just now if that's OK," she replied gently.

"But they just got in all the new Suburbans! You don't mean to say you don't enjoy looking at cars with me, do you? I mean, this is practically like going on a date, but it's free!"

"Dave, I love to spend time with you. But car lots just get a little old after a while, especially when we aren't even seriously looking for a car right now."

She clearly was not grasping the concept.

"Dale, you don't have to be planning to *buy* a new car to enjoy *looking* at them! It's fun to just imagine! To smell the smell of a sport utility vehicle with leather interior and tinted windows and antilock disc brakes for a mere $45,000 plus taxes, doc fees, licensing, and all those things they say real fast on the radio ads! This isn't about shopping, this is about fun!"

"Well, after three car lots in five days, I think I've had just about all the 'fun' I can take for this week," she said. "How about if we limit it to once a month, and you can take the kids or a friend if you want to go more often?"

Vital Marriage Point: Marriage would be much more satisfying if women learned to compromise.

CHAPTER 19

Falling Your Way to the Top

The National Park Service calls it a "cinder cone," not only because it is an apt description of this particular type of volcano but also because calling it "nature's version of a treadmill where you can walk for hours and hours and actually move backwards" won't fit on a sign. Also, printing such a blunt message might drive off visitors and thus severely cut down on a main source of Park Service employee amusement—watching hapless tourists scamper pointlessly forward like little hamsters on their exercise wheel.

When you tell the Park Service ranger that you are planning to climb the cinder cone, he will reply, "I was on the peak last week. It is a beautiful view."

He will leave out the little detail that he got to the top via helicopter.

A cinder cone is a mountain formed entirely of porous, lightweight, scratchy rocks that were formed when hot gas and molten rock were belched into the air by the young earth. The young earth did not bother to say, "Excuse me," either. That's one of the problems with youngsters. No manners.

You don't really climb these puffs of coarse rock. You slip and claw your way forward, literally moving two steps forward and one step back.

We were vacationing in Lassen Volcanic National Park in the summer of 1999 and found ourselves crawling, slipping, wheezing, and panting our way to the top of what amounts to several million truckloads of the kind of rock you find in the bottom of a gas barbecue grill, but without all the grease.

It is a brutal climb.

It got to the point where I was finally gasping for breath, my legs were screaming in pain, and I did not feel I could go on.

"I don't think I can make it," I wheezed. "You may have to send for a rescue team."

"I don't think they dispatch emergency personnel until you've climbed more than ten feet," Mark said.

This was not a good sign.

Forty-five minutes later . . .

"I don't think we've made any progress," Brad finally gasped, pausing to wipe his brow.

"We're doing great," Dale replied unconvincingly.

But Brad had a point. The trail snaked around the mountain, and what lay before us looked just like what went behind us. There were no landmarks, no trees, no shrubs, no outcroppings: just the stark sky against the uniform chunks of fifty-cent-size puffs of cinder rock. I couldn't tell if we had moved 500 feet or 50.

We pressed on.

Stupid little arguments broke out: Whose turn was it to carry the backpack, who was going too fast or too slow, who was kicking up too much dust, why did we start this climb in the first place, and can't we just turn back now?

The boys were clearly growing frustrated.

"Would you PLEASE stop whining?" they snapped at me.

Two steps forward, one step back, as volcanic dust filled our nostrils.

It had been about a one-hour hike just to get to the base of the cone. Not a particularly arduous incline under normal circumstances, but made much more difficult by the finely crushed cinders underfoot. If you have ever walked on a coarse sand beach, sinking with each step, just imagine that beach at a sloping angle and you can imagine what the preliminary trail was like. Then imagine climbing a skyscraper-size pile of rocks at a 45-degree angle.

On our way to the base of the cone, we met a worn but smiling fellow hiker who was returning from the peak.

"Did you make it to the top?" Dale asked her.

The hiker nodded, adding, "It's a spectacular view."

But halfway to the top, the view is not spectacular. The view is the tops of your hiking boots as you labor forward, head down, sucking in an atmosphere that is 8,000 feet higher than where you live.

Step, slide. Step, slide. Step, slide.

Forward and back.

Profit and loss.

Inhale and exhale.

Pressing on, we eventually see a small sprig of green up around a bend. It is a small bush, a landmark, a fixed point by which to measure our progress. Other small bushes slowly appear, proving we are moving forward.

We have just about HAD IT with this climb—and we are suddenly, surprisingly at the top. And it is, in fact, a spectacular view. To the west looms the peak of Mount Lassen, still an active volcano. It erupted in 1914—a mere snap of the fingers in geologic time—and the dramatic event was captured in grainy black-and-white photographs taken from fifty miles away.

The acrid odor of sulfur is carried by the clouds of steam that still hiss from the side of Lassen. The fumes are overwhelming, almost rivaling what happens when our kids take off their shoes after climbing all day.

To the east lie the Painted Dunes—smooth rolling hills splashed in hues of wheat and burgundy. Two deep-blue small lakes flank the dunes.

Sheer, utter beauty.

We approach the rim of the cinder cone, which drops down at a severe angle, and peer into the bowl.

"Cool!" the boys exclaim at the same moment and begin scrambling down the slopes and into the very belly of the beast.

I am suddenly reminded of a time, decades ago, when my parents drove our family out to the Midwest to visit relatives. We arrived late at night in the middle of a tornado warning.

I was petrified.

"How can you stand to live in a *tornado* zone?" I asked my cousin.

He just shrugged.

"It's no big deal."

"You're crazy," I replied.

"My mom said you live by a volcano! Talk about crazy!" he retorted.

"They aren't nearly as dangerous as the earthquakes," I replied.

After debating the relative merits of our regional natural hazards, we tried to agree upon the location of a risk-free place to live. But once you factor in threats from floods, hurricanes, forest fires, tornadoes, earthquakes, and tidal waves, not to mention nuclear missiles and those irritating Wisk detergent commercials, we came to the somber conclusion that there is no such thing as a safe place to live.

Even if you escape the aforementioned list of dangers, there are myriad hazards ranging from car accidents to criminals.

Life is not safe.

Life is not an easy climb.

Life is often two steps forward, one step back.

Dale and I have friends who have had children born with debilitating physical conditions, children who have died, or the one-two punch of *both*. We have friends who have said "I do" at the altar, and then one of them decided, years later, "I don't." We have friends who have been stricken with cancer, who have suffered staggering financial losses due to circumstances beyond their control, and others who have lost their mates.

We are all scrambling up the mountain of life, slipping and sliding as we go, sometimes relishing the view, sometimes so exhausted we don't think we can take another step, sometimes wondering if the whole thing is just going to blow up on us.

Wherever you find yourself in that mix of possibilities,

here are a few broad tips for climbing, and for life:

1. *Don't climb alone.* Even if circumstances are such that you can't climb with your mate, find someone to share the trip. A good friend will go along with you.

2. *Take time out to catch your breath.* You are in a long-distance event, not a sprint. Don't burn yourself out. Pace yourself.

3. *Sometimes progress is measured in inches, not feet.* The direction you want to be going is *forward*. Even if you can't see the progress happening, it is taking place as long as you keep doing the kinds of things that classify as positive rather than negative.

4. *You can do more than you think you can.* "The journey of a thousand miles begins with a single step."* Don't get overwhelmed by the size of the mountain. No one is asking you to pole-vault your way to the top. You'll be amazed at the progress you'll make if you just keep taking positive steps.

5. *The view at the top is, indeed, spectacular, and worth all the effort.* Don't forget that Moses climbed his mountain and found God at the top. As you slip-slide your way forward—hot, tired, and sore—He is *rushing* downslope to meet you.

> *I lift up my eyes to the hills—*
> *where does my help come from?*
> *My help comes from the Lord,*
> *the Maker of heaven and earth.*
> *He will not let your foot slip—*

---

*I don't know who said this, or I would give appropriate credit. I think it was some ancient Chinese person, because I saw it in a fortune cookie.

he who watches over you will not slumber;
indeed, he who watches over Israel
will neither slumber nor sleep.
>   —Psalm 121:1–4

CHAPTER 20

Follow the Leader

He *looked* like a normal minister, and as he administered our wedding vows he *sounded* like a normal minister, but John Lipscomb was most certainly *not* your normal minister, unless your definition of normal minister includes attacking a member of the congregation with a plate of steamed vegetables.

Well, perhaps "attacking" is too strong a term. But it was, at minimum, a very *forceful* use of Brussels sprouts, and I seriously doubt that such an unorthodox use of a vegetable would pass muster with most church bylaws. Unfortunately for me, John Lipscomb was not big on adhering to church bylaws.*

I was sixteen years old when I met Pastor Lipscomb.

"Hello, pastor," I said.

---

*This nonconformity to typical church protocol also helps explain the absence of certain attendance rolls during John's tenure. Years after he left the pastorate, he received a concerned call from the person responsible for denominational records: "With all due respect, sir, 'quite a few' is NOT an official annual Sunday school tally!"

"Hello, high school student," he replied.

"What?" I asked.

"If you are going to call me by a title, I am going to call you by one," he replied in his southern drawl. "In fact, I think I'll start calling everyone by their occupation instead of their name. Look, here comes Trucker Smith!"

From then on, he was just "John."

He loved to invest his time in young, zealous, clueless young people like me and my friends and my future spouse. He was the most unconventional, brilliant, unpredictable, amicable, confusticating pastor to have ever barreled into the tiny community church like a tornado with a Bible.

"His name is not 'Thee' and He is not impressed when people pray, 'Oh, what a great Thee Thou art.' "

John was the barbecuer of sacred cows.

EXAMPLE:

CHURCH MEMBER: "Pastor John, I have a real burden for my neighbor. Would you come and talk to him about his soul?"

ANSWER: "No."

CHURCH MEMBER: "No? You're a minister and you are NOT going to talk to my neighbor about his soul?"

ANSWER: "Correct. He's your neighbor, not mine. And you have the burden for him, not me. Look up John 3:16 and go talk to him."

This is not to say John was shy about sharing the faith. On the contrary, having been rebuffed in his effort to gain permission to come onto a local college campus to preach the gospel, it suddenly occurred to him that he could just enroll and say anything he wanted. He signed up for biology, where for a class project he painstakingly assembled the bones of a squirrel and a turkey and unveiled an undiscovered evolutionary form.

The class stared at it, dumbfounded.

"It's a water bat," he announced.

"Mr. Lipscomb, that is nothing more than a ridiculous concoction of assorted bones."

"So's the Piltdown man," he groused, and challenged both students and faculty to consider whether it took more faith to believe in a Supreme Being or to buy the argument that random, thoughtless forces produced the universe and made possible the music of Bach.

John could anger people to the point that they sometimes threatened to do him bodily harm.

"Bring your lunch, it'll take a while," he would reply.

Confrontational when he felt the situation warranted it, he could also be amazingly soft-spoken and kind. Both John and his wife, Colleen, were neighborly and hospitable to a fault, and thus I and my high school buddies found ourselves crowded at the Lipscomb table sharing fried chicken with four Lipscomb kids.

I passed the Brussels sprouts without taking any.

"You need some greens," John said.

"I don't like them," I replied.

"Have you ever tried them?"

"Uh, no. But I know I don't like them. They look like yucky little shrunken cabbages."

"I think you need to eat some vegetables," he said.

John was an immense and muscular man who looked like the stereotypical kind of guy you would picture serving in the United States Marine Corps and joining in barroom brawls and crashing a pitcher of beer into a drill sergeant's head, which, as it turns out, was precisely his résumé before God wrestled him to the ground and pinned him.

"I'd eat them if I was you," advised five-year-old Michael Lipscomb.

"Why?" I retorted. "It isn't like he can *make* me if I . . ."

I was suddenly immobilized in a remarkably effective half nelson, my mouth was squeezed open by strong fingers, steamed Brussels sprouts filled my cheeks, and my head began rhythmically bobbing up and down as a powerful unseen force made me chew them up.

"Told ya," Michael said.

John had an IQ in the stratosphere. He studied the New Testament in its original language. His sermons could rival a course at any good seminary. He could easily have been a college professor or the minister of an enormous congregation, but his pastorate was in a tiny rural community of about nine hundred, with a median income well below the state average.

He said he was there because it was where "the Lord of glory" wanted him. He and Colleen had walked away from a six-figure income for the privilege of ministering to a tiny flock about as far away as you can get from the potential for career advancement.

And because of that decision, small-town kids like Dale and me got the chance to pepper him with questions and be profoundly changed by the insight and example of this extraordinarily gifted man and his gracious, sweet wife.

"Just follow the Lord" was John's signature comment. While good advice in general, it could be maddeningly ambiguous when you were after specific advice about a school, or a vocation, or even *driving directions*.

"Could you be a bit more specific?" I would ask him.

"I'm not your guru, and I'm not the Holy Spirit," he would reply. "Just follow the Lord."

"OK. How about if, instead of asking for advice, I just ask what *you* would do in my situation?" I replied.

"Well," he would muse. "Given what you've told me, if I were in your shoes, I'd just follow the Lord."

"*How*, exactly?!?"

"The best way you know how."

And he'd smile.

Even after he packed up his family and moved a couple thousand miles away, I kept in touch with them.

And when Dale and I decided to marry, it was natural to ask John to come back to perform the ceremony. He said he would be honored. And thus Dale and I found ourselves saying "I do" as John hovered over us, beaming like a proud father.

And still we kept in touch over the years that followed.

The news of his death in the fall of 1998 hit me with the force of a truck. It was a heart attack, as he played a round of golf with one of his many friends. He was gone before the ambulance reached the hospital.

We could not make it back to the funeral. We sent a card to Colleen and the family and tried to express in a few sentences how much we cared about her and how much we missed John. I tried to sit down a week later and write something more substantive, but I tore it up after three failed attempts.

I let it rest and tried a few months later. It also ended up in the trash.

Ditto, six months later.

How do you nail down on paper just what someone like John means to you? Because right off the bat there is no such thing as someone "like" John. When you are sixteen years old and you have been saying "grace" over your meals since you were a little kid, and John takes you and your friends out to a restaurant, and "grace" becomes a ten-minute prayer of thanks and adoration to the Lord of glory, and the waitress keeps coming back to see if he is done yet (the answer, fifteen times in a row, was no), it starts to sink in that "grace" is a bigger deal than you thought it was.

And when a preacher/scholar is willing to drive ninety miles round trip once a week to come and teach a group of kids about Jesus, it dawns on you that the message must be really important if someone is going to pour that kind of energy and commitment into it.

And when Dale and I realized that this guy could have done anything and been anything, but that his life revolved around loving God and serving people, we saw a model for our own lives.

We just want to follow the Lord the best way we know how.

CHAPTER 21

The Gift That Keeps On Giving (Unfortunately)

One year I gave my wife what had become an annual Christmas tradition—five more jolly pounds of me. Sadly, Dale's holiday spirit had been declining for several straight years in a row.

"Are you *serious?* You're going on a diet?" she grinched as I stepped off the bathroom scales.

Some women lack an appreciation for Yuletide traditions.

I thus found myself nibbling on thin crackers and swilling down a powdered mix that was supposed to taste like a chocolate shake augmented with "roughage and minerals," by which the manufacturer apparently meant "sawdust and dirt."

Intellectually, I knew Dale was right about my weight. If I kept up my bad habits I would reach my sixty-fifth birthday weighing as much as the USS *Nimitz* and also facing the very real danger of having military aircraft try to land on me when I went swimming in the ocean.

I also knew that if I was going to succeed in my quest to slim down, I would need all the moral support I could get, including the assistance of my son Mark, who was just three years old at the time and was *seriously* into Oreos and other Epicurean delights that were now forbidden to me.

"Mark, I have been eating too many goodies, and if I keep it up I might get sick. So can you help Daddy resist the cookies?"

Mark immediately ran to the kitchen, climbed up on the counter, grabbed an Oreo from the jar, and jumped up and down while squealing, "Neener, neener, neener! You can't have some!"

This episode did not quite make the grade as one of those "precious moments" that make parenting so rewarding. Don't count on someone making one of those little porcelain statuettes out of the scene.

But with that show of support, I began my diet.

Dale tried to be chipper and upbeat about the ordeal, but even when she put the best china on the table and lit candles for dinner, there was no way she could hide the fact that my plate featured steamed birch bark and one square centimeter of chicken (skinless and broiled, lest there be any danger of retaining any actual flavor). And the semi-darkness of the candlelight did nothing to hide the scent of lasagna wafting up from Mark's plate.

I stared ruefully at my "dinner" while Dale tried to pretend she was engrossed in studying a map of the United States, but I suspected she was simply trying to hide her plate from me.

"I can't live on this!" I groused.

"I never knew Ohio had such sharp edges!" Dale exclaimed from behind her map.

I turned to Mark and whispered, "Good news, buddy! As a special reward for being three, Daddy will eat your bread crusts for you tonight!"

"But Mommy says I have to always eat my crusts," he said.

"Since when do *you* care what Mommy says?! You NEVER eat your bread crusts!" I hissed.

"I like them now," he replied, stuffing them into his mouth.

Fortunately for him, state law at that time forbade selling your preschooler to the circus.

Summoning courage and stamina I didn't know I possessed, I endured immeasurable levels of deprivation and stuck to the diet. It was awful. All I could think about was food. I was literally drooling over the Whopper ads on TV. When I finally climbed back onto the scales, I was shocked to see that I had actually *gained* an ounce. All that suffering and agony for *nothing!* Clearly I was one of those unlucky souls who had a glandular condition that made weight loss virtually impossible.

"It isn't working! I weigh more than I did before I went though all this torture! Oh well, at least we know that there is no point in carrying on with this torment," I said to Dale.

She stared at me coldly with no trace of sympathy.

"You have to be on it for more than forty-five minutes to notice any progress. And don't harbor any hopes that I missed the Snickers wrapper in the glove compartment of your car," she replied.

Vital Marriage Point: Trust is a critical component of any marriage, but this important facet of your relationship will be severely strained if your wife doesn't have enough faith in you to believe that someone else, perhaps a foreign agent, is responsible for the box of Hostess Ho Ho's under your side of the bed.

So I went back to weeks of birch strips and "breast molecule of chicken" as my main staples. And they had all the taste of staples, too, but with less iron.

Call it a revelation, but it finally dawned on me that the calorie spirits have played a cruel joke on everyone who has ever poured skim milk on his morning bowl of unsweetened puffed rice.

As we all learned in high school science class, we live in a closed universe. This means that calories, like energy, cannot escape, they can merely be transformed. Or as a physicist would put it, for every Arnold Schwarzenegger, there is an equal and opposite Danny DeVito. So when someone else plays a game of tennis, some poor slob like me is getting *their* calories.

Imagine the public reaction once this information is widely disseminated.

TV NEWSPERSON: "There were several grisly new incidents today of joggers being deliberately run over by enraged women driving Chrysler station wagons. Also in the news, a mob of incensed Weight Watchers adherents descended on Capitol Hill today, demanding enactment of the Equal Pounds for Equal Height bill, which was introduced by Congressman Fred 'Love Handles' Merkowitz. And over at the U.S. Olympic Training Center, pandemonium ensued when a portly humor writer attempted to force-feed Sugar Babies to members of the U.S. Swim Team."

Having discovered this law of nature, I decided to celebrate the momentous event by indulging in an Oreo.

I was just sneaking my hand into the jar when Mark walked into the kitchen.

"You aren't s'posed to have any!" he exclaimed, eyes the size of baseballs.

"I'm only having one," I explained. "Five or six at the most."

"I'm telling Mom."

"I'll give you twenty dollars," I implored him.

"MOOOOOOMMMMMMMMMMMMMMMMM!"

I crammed the Oreo into my mouth and began chomping as fast as I could.

Mark burst into tears.

"You aren't *s'posed* to!" he cried.

Uh-oh.

Suddenly this was no longer an issue of simply sneaking a cookie. In the eyes of a three-year-old kid, Daddy doing something he knows he should not do, even something as seemingly insignificant as lapsing on a diet, is a moral failure right up there with violating the Ten Commandments.

"Cum ovfer heer," I mumbled to Mark, and allowed him to watch me as I scraped the mushy cookie out of my mouth and into the kitchen trash can.

I rinsed out my mouth, got down on his level, and let him play "dental inspection."

"I'm sorry, Mark. Daddy gave in to temptation, but I am very sorry. The cookie is *allllll* gone. Is it OK now?"

He smiled, nodded, gave me a hug, and then scampered up the chair and onto the counter and grabbed an Oreo, scraped the filling across his teeth and sang, "Neener, neener, neener! You can't have some!"

If there had been a circus in town that week, this kid would have found himself cleaning out the elephant stalls.

Dale and I continued to make failed attempts at dieting for the next decade plus. But one day she attended a class called "Weigh Down Workshop"* which, at its core, teaches two fundamental concepts: (1) eat only when you are actually hungry, and (2) eat only until you are comfortably full.

"This just makes so much sense," Dale said after the first class. "No measuring little cups of this and that, no restrictive menu plans, no more terrible, tasteless food. You just eat when you are truly hungry and quit when you are full."

She started losing weight, and felt better almost at once. On the downside, she blew my Danny DeVito theory to smithereens. I was now without excuse. My weight is an issue of self-control, plain and simple.

"Dave, I want to grow old with you. You need to take this seriously," Dale said gently. "The old saying about having 'too much of a good thing' applies to you, too."

There is an old hymn that goes, "All to Jesus I surrender..."

"All" as in "all our excuses."

And all our extra pounds.

I told Dale that next Christmas, I plan to give her ten less pounds of me.

"That's the nicest gift you've never given me," she replied. "I can hardly wait to not get it."

---

*by Gwen Shamblin

What's Good for the Goose Is Bad for the Gander

"You *have* to get a mammogram," I told Dale. "This is *not* optional. It is a basic part of maintaining your health. Good grief, we *know* people who have contracted breast cancer!"

"I know," she admitted reluctantly. "But the exam is just so awkward and uncomfortable."

"Get used to it," I replied tersely. "It's for your own good. I'm not going to risk your health over mild discomfort. I don't want to lose you to some preventable disease!"

It took some serious coaxing on my part, but she finally agreed. I breathed a huge sigh of relief when the results were negative. She was given a perfect bill of health.

"Dave, when was the last time *you* had a complete physical?" Dale asked later that evening.

"Well, technically, at birth," I said defensively.

"Then to quote someone famous, 'Get used to it,' " she said.

"But I'm perfectly healthy," I protested.

"This is a basic part of maintaining your health," Daley replied tersely. "I'm not going to risk your health over mild discomfort. I don't want to lose you to some preventable disease!"

Vital Marriage Point: Quoting a spouse's own advice back to him or her is *really* irritating, especially when it is true and completely applicable.

So I made an appointment for a complete physical exam—based upon my assumption that no doctor gives your prostate gland a second thought until you are at least forty (which I was not, not that it did me much good).

Before you could say "Jack Robinson" or "Hey, why are you putting on surgical gloves?" or "There must be some kind of mistarrghhh!" I was half undressed and gripping the examining table for dear life while a **complete stranger** was apparently attempting to probe my tonsils via the scenic route.

"How much did my wife pay you to do this?" I demanded, looking wildly around the room for the *Candid Camera* crew.

"Your wife cares more about your health than you do," he replied. "Now cough a few times."

"How was it?" Dale asked when I got home.

"No worse than having a large Maytag appliance shoved up your nose," I replied. "At least it's over. Thank heaven, I'll never have to do that again."

"That's where you're wrong," chirped Dale. "This is now an annual event, just like Thanksgiving."

"It's a lot more like April 15," I grumbled.

"Try to think of it as character-building," Dale advised.

"Then you have to get a mammogram every year!" I retorted.

"Deal!" she grinned.

Another Vital Marriage Point: Although women will say they are just concerned about their husband's health, the *real* reason they insist on yearly prostate exams is to retaliate for childbirth.

Out of curiosity, I dusted off a copy of the *American Medical Association Family Medical Guide* and flipped it open to the section on the prostate gland. Three sentences into the text, it blandly revealed that "the exact function of the prostate gland is unclear." I am not kidding. It's on page 586.

"I'm supposed to allow doctors to annually go up the down staircase, and they don't even know what this gland does? And this is legal?" I complained to Dale.

"It's for your own good," she replied.

As Yogi Berra once said, "It's like *déjà vu* all over again."

Reading on, the revised and updated medical book noted that cancer of this mystery gland is the third most common cause of cancer deaths in the United States, surpassing even dinner at the Kevorkian home.

It isn't that the prostate cancer itself kills you, but rather the cancer that spreads from the prostate to the bones.

"By the age of eighty," the medical book stated, "virtually every male has it, although usually it is only visible with the aid of a microscope." (This may help explain why the exam is so uncomfortable.)

In the event that Mr. Prostate decides to invite some cancer cells over for a casual evening of plotting a guy's demise, doctors are split over the issue of treatment. Some feel that a cancer that remains confined to the prostate gland and which causes no symptoms should simply be monitored to ensure that it is not spreading to the bones.

While avoiding surgery is a real plus, the downside is that you get to have LOTS of prostate exams for the rest of your life. Your colon will experience more traffic than the New Jersey Turnpike.

Other doctors favor removing the gland, yet my trusty medical book points out that there are, and I quote, "unpleasant side effects," which I am **not** going to go into any detail about other than to note that I could not sleep for three days after I read about them.

A third alternative, favored by millions of men, is to purchase substantial wads of life insurance and avoid physical exams like you would avoid a convention of enraged NOW activists.

But the bottom line (so to speak) is that the Bible specifically notes that once you are married you are no longer free to make unilateral decisions about your body.

"The wife's body does not belong to her alone but also to her husband. In the same way, the husband's body does not belong to him alone but also to his wife" (1 Corinthians 7:4).

This is God's version of checkmate—you each have the right to make sure your mate gets checked.

CHAPTER 23

For Better or for Worse, for Richer or for Poorer

My father taught me at a very young age that all work has dignity, and that as long as you work hard at it, there is no job too low to take pride in unless you are a trial lawyer, in which case you are lower than crabgrass, which at least produces oxygen.

I have held a wide variety of jobs over the years. Among other things, I have worked in a dairy, stocked shelves at a grocery store, written for a newspaper, and sold cameras. Currently I serve as an aide to a congressman, which means that, technically, I help run the United States government; and even though I only have a small role, you should nevertheless be alarmed.

My income has been all over the place, depending on what I was doing at the time. But I have found in each of those occupations that my dad's view of work really affected my own attitude about my various jobs.

Stocking shelves of disposable diapers late one

evening, I remarked to a co-worker, "You know, this town would be a LOT less pleasant place to live if you and I weren't here stocking these shelves every night—especially if we were standing downwind."

He turned to me and replied, "You're right. This job stinks. I'm going to go get drunk when we get off."

Something apparently got lost in the translation.

I have noticed over the years that the most upbeat people I have worked with have shared my dad's view of labor.

I was on a steam-drilling crew the summer I graduated from high school. Drilling is hard, gritty, demanding work. It is eight hours of sticking huge pipes down a hole, then pulling them back out to change a massive drill bit, getting sprayed with hot mud in the process, and putting the bit back down the hole to continue the operation.

In the predawn hours of the morning, my crew was on the deck of the rig going about our respective tasks while the pipe ate its way into the earth. My boss, Jay, leaned over to me and asked, "Do you know what we do for a living?"

I frowned, then replied, "We drill holes, looking for steam."

"Nope," he said, pointing to the horizon. "See that glow coming from the city over there? What activates those streetlights?"

"Electricity," I replied, bracing for the punch line.

"Right. We turn steam into electricity for all those people. Can you imagine not having electricity? We're making life better for a couple hundred thousand people. *That's* what this job is about."

I suddenly realized that no punch line was coming.

Standing there beneath the stars, the glare of the deck lights illuminating our mud-caked clothes, tired as dogs, we smiled at each other. Many guys felt trapped by the work, seeing nothing but hard, repetitive labor and a whole lot of mud. The money—and it was *good* money— was the only thing that kept them coming back to the job. But my boss saw purpose, and dignity, and even *public service* in his work. That's why I can easily remember the conversation even though it has been more than two decades since it took place.

Attitude is everything.

I think it is super important for people to feel a sense of purpose and dignity in their work, even if the work seems unattractive on the surface. My dad was a paper-maker for most of his working life. It is not a particularly glamorous job to turn wood chips into paper. But because of people like him, you can hold this book in your hands. Where would we be without paper?

Because my dad made paper for a living, our family had a roof over our heads and all the other stuff we needed—and even stuff we wanted, like a boat, so we could ski almost every weekend during the summer. It was honorable, important work.

One of the things I have always appreciated about my wife is that she has always valued whatever job I held. She took the marriage vow concept of "for richer or for poorer" quite literally. No matter what our income or what kind of work I was doing at a particular point in our life, she just rolled with it.

She wanted to help me achieve my potential, and that included getting me back to college so I could finish up my degree, but it was always in terms of supporting me, not making me feel like a failure for earning a modest income. She was my cheerleader, except she didn't use pom-pons or stand on the top of one of those human pyramids.

The real challenge was convincing her that *her* work was valuable and important, because for several years her work consisted of taking care of our two very active toddlers. Early in our marriage we decided that when we had kids, Dale would stay home with them. While this sounded great in theory, it was tremendously difficult in practice. Dale, an incredibly social person, suddenly found herself largely isolated at home with a colicky baby.

Not a lot of glamour there, folks. On the contrary, there is a lot of hard work: diapers, drool, and exhaustion. Sure, there is incredible sweetness and bonding as well, but let's not pretend for a moment that raising small children is a picnic.*

It is a monumental task for a new mom even to get a shower. Some days I would get home from work to find Dale still in her bathrobe. She would burst into tears and say, "I look like a hospital patient, and the only productive thing I have done all day is clean the toilet."

Meanwhile, every message coming out of Madison Avenue at that time communicated that truly successful women dressed like Cher and worked in corporate offices. And when other women asked Dale, "Do you work?" she looked dejected and replied no.

This *really* bugged me.

"Dale, you are doing the most incredibly difficult and

---

*Or if it *is* a picnic, there are jars of strained carrots involved and vivid orange baby barf.

important work in the world! You are raising *our kids!* Who else is going to love them like you do?" I would say in exasperation. "Besides, things will get better. Just hang in there."

Pep talks need to be a BIG part of a woman's day when she is the mother of young children.

And when I would occasionally get bummed out because I felt that I was spinning my wheels stocking shelves in a grocery store, Dale would say, "Hey, you are taking care of our family! That's a big deal! Besides, things will get better. Just hang in there."

We were in this thing together—for better or for worse, for richer or for poorer. Pep talks work both ways.

And even though our tasks were substantially different, our work has always been useful and filled with meaning.

Even now, in my latest occupation as a humor writer, I am proud to say that I produce . . . um . . . uh . . . well . . . now that I really think about it, strictly speaking, I don't produce *anything* useful. I mean, you can't produce energy from my books unless you burn them.

Whoa, this is *depressing!*

CHAPTER 24

Ten Brilliant and Insightful Marriage Tips for Guys That Will Get You Out of Trouble for Just About Any Stupid Thing You May Do

Please note that this book is sold by weight, not by content. Some content may have settled during shipping and handling. So if this chapter looks a bit light, I will just use the same excuse you find on your box of cornflakes.

1. Whenever you break something expensive, merely claim that the kids were . . .

2. If you accidentally back the car into the fence, especially if she warned you that you were getting too close, you just . . .

3. If you forget her birthday, again, make sure that . . .

4. If you neglect to write down a few ATM trans-

actions, and she comes home from the store looking *really* unamused, you'd better . . .

5. If you were the last one to drive the car, and she runs out of gas six blocks after pulling out of the driveway, you can get expedited passport service by simply . . .

6. When your wife gets very emotional because she discovers her first gray hair, and you respond by making an amusing comment about getting "senior discounts," you can regain most of your limb function by . . .

7. If it is a Monday, and you agree to go on a date next Saturday, make sure you clarify whether "next Saturday" means "the Saturday that comes next" or "the Saturday of the next week," or you'll discover that . . .

8. Although your wife may say she wishes you would be more "spontaneous," if you, on a whim, invite a bunch of guys over for a barbecue without first telling her . . .

9. And if you invited them over, thinking that "next Saturday" meant "the Saturday of the next week," you'll find that the recliner is much more comfortable if you stuff a pillow in the . . .

10. While all unintended carpet fires are cause for concern, if you strategically relocate some of the living room furniture while she is gone shopping she may think you were just trying to help redecorate the . . .

CHAPTER 25

In Sickness and in Health, Till Death Does Its Part

If we really thought through the implications of the wedding vows, it could very well unnerve us to the point that we would be *extremely* cautious before we said "I do," perhaps delaying marriage until we are more confident and mature . . . and in our late eighties.

Frankly, when you think about them, the vows are scary enough to send us shrieking down the street late at night dressed only in our pajamas and a robe—a severe reaction that is usually reserved for the clinically insane or those who suddenly realize it is April 15 and they have only twenty minutes to get their tax return down to the post office and still get it stamped on time.*

"I never thought that much about our vows before the accident," admitted my friend Nick one day after we finished a several-mile bike ride near Lake Siskiyou.

---

*I made it.

I glanced over at the travel trailer he and Sandra use when they go camping. It has a ramp instead of steps, and the door has been modified to accommodate the wheelchair that has been a part of their life since 1977 when a freak accident spun their world upside down.

The words "in sickness and in health" take on an entirely new dimension when "sickness" is a whole lot more than a bout with the flu.

But if you think about it, those vows encompass *all* health problems, including the possibility of your spouse suffering a crippling traffic accident a year after you got married, which is precisely what happened in the case of Nick and Sandra.

Standing at the altar, saying, "I do," a life-changing car crash is the last thing either of them expected would intrude into their life.

But *no one* expects this kind of tragedy. We know that bad stuff happens all the time, but deep down, we count on it happening to someone *else*. This is an intellectual self-defense mechanism we use so that we are not paralyzed by fear.

But when we take our marriage vows, even though they are couched in language designed to be acceptably poetic for the big occasion, you can't help but notice the jarring words "sickness," "worse," and "death."

The vows mean that you are betting the farm, biting the bullet, putting all your eggs in one basket, burning your bridges behind you, and even swallowing the whole enchilada, "until death do you part."

This means that you can be young and in love, starting a new life with the mate of your dreams, and the fairy tale can get rudely interrupted by the sound of screeching metal and shattering glass. And then a wheelchair can be parked by your bed.

You took some serious vows.

Did you mean them?

Nick explained that, deep down, he did not consider the vows particularly binding at the time he uttered them. As far as he was concerned, they were more poetry than promise.

Sandra had an entirely different point of view. She believed deeply that the vows were binding on *both* of them, and the issue of whether Nick had seriously thought through the ramifications of the vows was not terribly persuasive to her.

So when Nick broached the subject of ending their marriage, Sandra didn't buy it for a moment.

"I guess I just expected her to want out," Nick said, seated back into his wheelchair after maneuvering out of his hand-cranked three-wheel racing bike. "Most couples split up after this kind of accident."

Nick had to learn to do almost everything in a new way. His driving instructor's first lesson for Nick consisted of the following observation: "Nick, the first thing you need to understand is that your wife is going to leave you."

So Nick decided to make it easy on her.

"I told her I would understand if she wanted a divorce," Nick said.

To which Sandra replied, "I meant my vows."

Nick waited for the shoe to drop.

That was more than twenty years ago, and there has been no sound of falling footwear.

"It just rolled a big load off my shoulders when it sunk

in that she was really sticking with me," he grinned.

And that is precisely the point. God intends the vows to bring at least some certainty to an uncertain world. The vows are intended to anchor us in the assurance that marriage is for life. God does not abandon us when the going gets rough, and He does not want us to abandon each other, either. The vows are merely an extension of what God has committed himself to in His love relationship with us.

Love is not always warm and easy, with the cross of Christ serving as Exhibit A.

I know a woman named Laura who was diagnosed with breast cancer the day after celebrating her first wedding anniversary with Michael. This cancer was *bad*. Laura endured several doses of *intense* chemotherapy, which by definition means she was horribly nauseous and vomiting *every few hours* for nine or ten days at a time.

She lost all her hair.

She lost a breast.

Here they were, newlyweds, looking death in the face.

Put yourself in Michael's shoes, guys. You get married with a certain expectation or at least a hope of how your life will be. Usually that vision does not include kneeling in the bathroom next to your cancer-ravaged wife as she grips the toilet bowl and pukes for days on end.

Here is a short passage Laura penned about this horrific event: "Although I didn't know it at the time, there came a day shortly after my third treatment when Michael just couldn't take it anymore. So he lashed out at both God and his sister in anger and frustration. 'It's not fair,' he insisted. 'I didn't sign up for this.'

" 'Yes, you did,' his sister Sheri gently reminded him.

'I heard you: "For better or for worse; in sickness and in health." '

"Michael honored his vows then and now. Even throughout the entire breast reconstruction process. Or as we called it, the 'build-a-breast' route (sort of like Legos, except the pieces don't snap together."*

Laura jokes about it now. But it wasn't funny when she was hooked up to an IV, getting loaded with chemo, and wondering if she would live to celebrate another anniversary. And the biggest reason she can still laugh is that not only did she make it, but *they* made it. The vows prevailed, like a lighthouse standing its ground in a hurricane.

There has been a trend over the past several decades for couples to break with tradition and write their own wedding vows. In many cases, this is a way to make the ceremony more meaningful and personal. But in some instances, it also seems as though the couple is trying to carve out loopholes big enough to steer a battleship through.

They'll promise to stay together "as long as we both shall love" or "as long as we continue to grow" or "unless something icky happens, then I'm outta here."

They don't come right out and say that last one, but the first two are simply code words for the third.

Well, God isn't buying it. Even if we craft vows that leave all kinds of escape hatches, God still views our relationship as binding the moment we set up house together. "Until *death* do you part" is simply a restatement of something Jesus said.

---

*Taken from Laura Jensen Walker, *Dated Jekyll, Married Hyde* (Minneapolis: Bethany House Publishers, 1997). Thanks, Laura! For a fuller treatment of this subject, see her new book, *Thanks for the Mammogram* (New York: Fleming H. Revell, 2000).

Love—real love—risks all for the sake of the beloved. Love makes itself vulnerable by inextricably connecting itself to the loved one. "I do" is shorthand for "come what may, I am with you."

We all crave that security, that love without loopholes. But the only way to have it is to give it.

Love is high-risk. You are signing a blank but nevertheless binding contract, and God only knows what is in store. *And He isn't saying.* He gives us life one day at a time, or we would be whimpering in the closet or locked in an asylum.

One of the most terrifying episodes of my life began with a small dot on Dale's forehead. The strange little dot kept growing over the course of three days.

Initially Dale viewed it as an embarrassing but merely cosmetic problem. I was worried and insisted she go see the doctor.

He gave her some antibiotics.

The dot continued to grow.

And grow.

One morning she woke up to find her forehead puffed up to the point that she could not fully open her eyes.

"I look like a Klingon from *Star Trek,*" she quipped nervously.

I called the doctor. He said to bring her in right away.

We walked into his office; he took one look at her, and said, "Which hospital do you prefer?"

"What?" we said.

"I want you admitted within the next twenty minutes," he said, picking up the phone. "We are going to start you on some very powerful intravenous antibiotics. We don't want this infection moving into your brain."

That was thinly veiled language for "we are trying to avoid brain damage."

My wife was facing potential brain damage, and they were going to put her in the hospital, and I could feel my pulse pounding like a team of horses.

In a blur that I don't quite remember, Dale was admitted, dressed in one of those awful gowns, and hooked up to bags of clear fluid that hung from stainless steel hooks.

I did all kinds of supportive stuff, said all kinds of supportive things. I was Mr. Calm. I drove home to pick up some things for her and stepped inside the door and collapsed to my knees in tears, begging God to somehow make it all turn out. I grabbed a phone and called a friend's house and tried to leave a message on the answering machine, but could only manage a few semi-intelligible words while I wept and choked.

What if her brain became damaged? What if she couldn't speak, or walk, or even remember who I was? *What if I lost her?*

I remembered our friend Judy, who broke a leg, got a blood clot, and died. If someone could die from a broken leg, *anything* could happen.

"Oh, God, please, please, please, please, please get her through this!"

I don't think I ever loved Dale more than I did at that moment as she lay in a hospital bed with her eyes puffed shut, looking worse than she had ever looked in her life.

The vows did not even enter my mind.

The very idea of "obligation" was not even on the radar screen. I was not checking the contract to see if this was covered.

I just knew that I loved her, and that come what may we were in this together.

She was in the hospital for several days as the antibiotics battled the infection. Day by day the swelling receded. She came through with flying colors. The doctor said there was *no* lasting effect from the infection.*

That awful event crystallized for me just how much we have indeed become "one" in our marriage. We cannot imagine *not* being together. As we have lived out our vows these many years, they have been quietly changing us in deep ways.

There were times early on when the stresses of life and marriage were so difficult that, for both of us, the obligation inherent in the vows loomed large in our minds. We gritted our teeth and worked through the issues, but it was neither romantic nor fun.

I used to think that God wanted us to always remain very conscious of keeping our vows. I now believe that what God really intends is that the longer we keep our vows, the less we have to think about them, because the ideals embodied in the vows become imbedded in our hearts and our souls. He wants the vows to become second nature.

The Bible explains that the laws of God are a tutor to lead us to Jesus. If Jesus takes hold of you—*really* takes hold—the rules are superfluous.

Likewise, I think the vows are a tutor to lead us to love. When love takes hold of you—*really* takes hold—the vows are superfluous.

---

*For the record, Dale claims that her brain *has* been seriously altered, but says it is from living with me the majority of her life.

If God handed you a "Get Out of Marriage Free" card, which would enable you to walk away from your marriage with no guilt, no obligation, and no negative consequences, and if you shudder at the very thought of this, and if you can imagine yourself tearing the card up in little pieces, you get the idea of what He is after.

The vows are your map, but love is your destination.

"Love never fails."

(1 CORINTHIANS 13:8)

CHAPTER 26

Redecorating Your Spouse

One of the little secrets Dale did not know about me prior to saying "I do" was that—and this was very hard for her to accept once it came to light—I truly, honestly, sincerely do *not* care where the furniture is placed. She thought I was being inexplicably rude or passive-aggressive, but I was actually only being deferential. Furniture placement ranks number two on my "Couldn't Care Less" list, right behind the outcome of the National Croquet Championship (if there is one, not that I care enough to find out).

We were moving into a new house, and we had a whole herd of our friends helping us, and Dale would keep coming to me to ask where I thought various pieces of furniture should be placed. I would keep replying, "Whatever you like." And she got exasperated.

"I need you to help me figure out the right arrangement!" she finally snapped. "And please don't keep saying you don't care. You need to care about *our* home!"

"I *do* care about our home," I said. "I just don't care where you put everything. Feel free. Just go with your emotions. I won't complain."

"Dave, I need you to help me make these decisions. I am exhausted from all this moving, and I don't think it is fair for you to just dump all the decisions on me."

"OK," I said with a sigh. "How about sticking the couch against the south wall."

"Are you just saying that to say it, or do you mean it?" she said suspiciously.

"I mean it! I think the couch would look great there!" I said.

"I don't," she replied. "I think the love seat should go there, and the couch should go by the front window."

"Then why did you ask me?" I grumped.

"I wanted your opinion," she replied.

Things went much smoother once I began providing options that she could veto. After the move was finished, the next big house-related issue was outside paint.

Back before we had even purchased the house, which was pale blue, Dale noted that we would need to repaint it so it would match.

"Match what?" I asked.

She heaved the same kind of big sigh she used to heave when the kids were little and I would dress them in what I thought were perfectly acceptable combinations of clothing, but which she insisted made them look like tiny circus clowns.

"The house color does not match the roof," she replied. "Can't you see it? It looks awful. I want you to agree that if we buy it, we paint it."

"OK," I shrugged. "But let's at least catch our breath.

Moving is a big undertaking in and of itself."

So we moved in, and one fateful Saturday while I was still unpacking boxes of books, she said, "Dave, we need to pick out some paint colors."

I got alarmed.

"Hon, it isn't like it's a crisis or anything," I said. "Good grief, I'm still unpacking my office! What's the rush?"

Her eyes narrowed.

"You promised we would paint the house," she said.

"Dale, we've only been moved in for, uh . . ."

"*Five years!*" Dale retorted.

"Wow. That explains that series of Christmas trees!" I exclaimed.

So we found ourselves down at the paint store looking at little chips of color.

"Dave, what do you think about . . ."

"Whatever you pick is fine," I said.

Oops.

"We are going to be living with these colors for probably the next decade," Dale said. "Would you *please* try to be helpful?"

She picked out several color combinations.

"We could do 'sage' for the trim and 'oyster' as the main color, or there's 'forest' and 'beach whispers' or, oh, I really like the contrast of 'grain' and 'Monterey,' " Dale said.

I looked at the paint chips.

"They all look identical," I replied, puzzled.

"Would you please *try* to be helpful?"

"I'm not kidding," I retorted. "I can't tell them apart!"

"I'll tell you what," Dale said. "Just pick out some colors you like, and we'll go from there."

So I picked out two colors from the prematched "Let the Experts Help You" brochure.

"How about these?" I said, handing the paper to Dale.

"Green and 'industrial off-white.' How daring," she replied dryly.

"I think they look great," I said.

And I meant it. They were real, solid colors you could figure out. But Dale said she wanted something more "subtle and nuanced," which is what happens when you marry someone whose hobby is painting watercolors.

So we went home with a couple of test pints of colors called "heather essence" and "sandpiper dreams."

I applied them to the side of our house.

She hated them both.

"They look diluted—almost sickly pale," she grimaced.

So back to the store we went, this time bringing home "muted jade" and "fleece."

She hated these, too.

Ditto for "seafoam" and "pyramid wash."

"They never look like the paint chips," she complained, very frustrated.

So we went back to the paint store once again and entered the bold new world of creating our own colors from scratch.

We did not name these colors, but if we did I would have chosen "we are going to die of old age in this store" and "I am about to scream." I believe that I distinctly saw the clerks diving for cover when we drove up for the fifth time, but they may have just simultaneously had seizures.

Dale was starting to get both embarrassed and depressed, which is a very bad combination that usually ends in tears. So I decided to make an executive decision.

"Let's just try the green and off-white and see what they look like," I said.

We drove home and I slapped these new colors on the test wall, which was starting to resemble a paintball firing range.

"It's perfect!" she beamed, giving me a big hug.

"So I was *right* all along?" I asked, already starting to gloat.

"Yes, but we didn't *know* you were right until we tried the other options, so it was all worth it," she grinned.

I still can't figure out if I was vindicated or vetoed.

CHAPTER 27

Having It All

Dale and I are blessed to own a several-hundred-acre ranch that includes orchards, a small lake, abundant wild flowers, scores of geese and ducks, a spectacular view of area mountains, and even a few miles of paved walking trails. When the weather is nice, we walk the trails together almost every day.

The spread demands quite a bit of upkeep, and the property taxes are staggeringly high, but we figure it is all worth it, especially since someone else does all the work and pays all the bills.

Strictly speaking, the ranch isn't "ours," in the sense that the title is not actually in our name, or in the name of our parents, or in the name of anyone we even know. If you want to get nitpicky about it, the ranch is actually owned by a private foundation, but they are kind enough to open up the grounds to the general public, which includes us. So since we get to enjoy it whenever we want, it is practically like we own it (although they would probably get a bit testy if we started getting our mail there).

All the benefits and none of the obligations! Talk about having it all!

I mean, let's suppose that the owners decided that the place was just way too much work, so they gave it to Dale and me.* Would we suddenly enjoy the hills more if we owned them? Would the mountains look any better, or the flowers any brighter, or the geese any geesier? Would the trails be more pleasant to walk? Is "geesier" even a word? I would never know the answers to these questions, because I would be strapped to a riding lawn mower for the rest of my life trying to keep the grass under control.

One of the virtues God has called us to embrace is "contentment," which I once heard a minister define as "wanting what you have."

Unfortunately, there is a multibillion-dollar industry dedicated to the task of making us lust for more, and *more*, and *MORE!!!* Madison Avenue rakes in *mountains* of money preying on our ego, our sense of inferiority, our sex drive, our greed, and even our stupidity, as exhibited by the ad campaign for KOOL cigarettes—a campaign that has long featured photos of robust Olympic-class athletes standing by their mountain bikes and looking at a water-fall *while holding cigarettes*.

I handed the magazine to Brad one day and asked, "What is the message here?"

He studied it, smiled, and said, "They are trying to make it look like smoking goes along with all this healthy

---

*For the sake of argument, let's say they were not the *brightest* owners in the world.

stuff like mountain biking and getting out in nature. But you can tell the models don't smoke because they don't have yellow teeth."

We were laughing at how STUPID this ad was and how they must think we were all idiots, when we both noticed the BMW automobile advertisement on the opposite page, and Brad's eyes bulged out, and he said, "Why can't *we* have a cool car like that?" which is EXACTLY what I was thinking as my greedometer pegged out at 100.

So even though I can see what they are trying to do, I am nevertheless susceptible to their slick marketing ploys because they are absolute geniuses at appealing to my covetousness.

The cigarette ads are not remotely tempting to me, but materialism is another story. I realize it is my moral obligation to fight this impulse, but it is, indeed, a fight. Every day on my way to work I pass by a real estate advertisement that urges me to "dream great dreams." The ad features a guy looking longingly at his "dream house," which appears to have more rooms than your average Holiday Inn. The house is *absurdly* large. Sure, it is architecturally beautiful, but so is Buckingham Palace—and who can afford the utility bills for either one of them unless you are, personally, the Princess of Wales? (In which case you *also* get stuck with Prince Charles as your roommate.)

You might need that house if you were running an orphanage, but I don't think the advertisement is catering to our charitable side. No, that ad—like so many others—screams, "Spend, spend, *spend* on yourself and all your dreams will come true! You DESERVE to plunge into an absolute festival of self-gratification and opulence—and you can even *charge* it, which is almost like having it for *free!*"

This advertisement is, in its own way, every bit as stupid as the KOOL cigarettes ad, with the exception that every time I see the picture of that absolutely ridiculous house *I want it!* I want it *all!* I want the yard, the 157 rooms, the pool the size of Lake Erie, the private art collection, and the wood-paneled cigar room, even though the smell of cigar smoke makes me violently ill and I would have to dash to the tastefully appointed 900-square-foot bathroom and lunge for the imported European toilet.

We Americans are particularly vulnerable to appeals to our greed because we are living in the most prosperous, advanced nation in the history of the world. All around us lays the attraction of *stuff*. A fundamental purpose of advertising is to create a desire for something we would otherwise think we could live without.

But, frankly, they don't have to work all that hard at it, because we are by nature prone to materialism. And unlike the peasants of the ancient world, who could only gaze with longing at the royal splendor that surrounded them, we have VISA cards.

But in exactly the same way that God tells us to control the temptations of sexual sin, gluttony, and anger, He tells us to control our lust for stuff, even going to the point of equating greed with idol worship.

Whoa.

So this materialism thing is serious. In fact, all the real marriage experts list financial issues and money as one of the big marriage killers. Couples get in debt way over their heads as they amass stuff, then fight about money because they are so stressed out. Or one partner makes unreasonable demands on the other to provide more and more money to acquire stuff or do expensive stuff. Or one of them is responsible and prudent about money, and one of them spends like a Massachusetts senator. In all these cases, the lust for stuff is crowding out the things God values, like selflessness, generosity, and contentment.

Dale and I have not conquered materialism, but we fight it. We try to take affirmative steps to overcome it. We have our share of stuff, and we have not taken a vow of poverty or moved into a monastery or anything, but we try to fight the good fight in several ways.

First, we give away part of our income. We think it is a powerful antidote to selfishness. It is also something God has stated He wants us to do.

Second, when one of us (usually me) is feeling particularly sucked in by the predominant worldview, we talk about it.

EXAMPLE:

ME: "Dale, the car needs a complete set of new tires. Rather than pouring that kind of money into the old beast, I calculated that for the price of the new tires, we could almost make an entire month's payment on that new sport utility vehicle, the Ford Extravaganza. I think this would be prudent stewardship, but I want to know if you think I might be blinded by materialism."

DALE: "Here's a glass of warm milk. Go take a nap."

ME: "But it has a CD player *and* a built-in Jacuzzi."

DALE: "Make that a long nap."

ME: "But this could be a ministry opportunity! The

Extravaganza is large enough that we could probably use it to open up a mobile orphanage. Did I mention it also has a built-in bowling alley?"

DALE: "You may actually want to hibernate for a month."

Third, I look for ways to periodically expose myself to poverty to jar myself back into the reality of just how good we have it. I have forced myself to read grim historic records of the Irish Potato Famine, for example. If you want to get a sense of how blessed you are today, no matter how financially struggling you may think you are, try reading about the suffering that has plagued much of the world for much of human history.

Fourth, our kids are plugged into a really good youth group that places a high value on service. They do clean-up work at the local rescue mission, they take ministry trips to nonvacation destinations like Watts, where they serve underprivileged kids and paint facilities, and they get challenged to take God's worldview seriously.

When Mark returned from the Watts trip, I asked him what big lesson he learned.

"A big house is not important," he said. "There are little kids down there who have *nothing*. If we all chipped in, we could do a lot to help them have a better life."

That is "dreaming great dreams," although it is not what the real estate marketing guys had in mind.

Fifth, we enjoy what we do not own, like the walking trails we use so often. We also like the ocean, the sunset, the stars, and the bright glow of the moon, and neither of us felt compelled to fall for the ad campaign by the people who actually tried to sell deeds to moon parcels. We may struggle with materialism, but we are not brain-dead.

Finally, even though our house sometimes feels a little cramped and our older-model cars have some quirks and noises that we find irritating, when I contemplate the fact that I am loved by the God who made the hills that I enjoy so much, and when I consider that I am deeply cherished by the woman who matters most to me in all the world, I realize that I am richer than most kings who have ever walked the earth. Plus, I don't have to pay the heating bill for 157 rooms or have Prince Charles as a roommate.

CHAPTER 28

The Gang's All Here!

He was built like a brick wall and he was heading toward me like a runaway freight train. His heavily tattooed arms bore grotesque emblems—a skull and crossbones, a swastika, a dragon. "SWP"—the acronym for a racist movement known as Supreme White Power—was emblazoned beneath his neck.

His eyes were locked onto me—and the Hispanic friend with whom I was speaking. I could see what was coming, and I braced myself for the inevitable.

Powerful arms simultaneously grabbed my friend and me and lifted us right off the floor.

"Group hug!" shouted Donny, beaming a smile as he scooped us up in a friendly, albeit stout, embrace. "Howya doin', brothers?"

Chalk up another one for God, I mused.

Here I was, a conservative Republican in wing-tip shoes, sandwiched in a bear hug between a Hispanic former gang member and a former white supremacist ex-convict covered in more ink than your daily newspaper. Under ordinary circumstances, this is *not* the mix of people you would invite to the same event unless the event involved a bailiff. But God does not operate under ordinary circumstances. He transforms them into extraordinary circumstances.

He positively delights in throwing together people from all backgrounds and walks of life to create relationships and friendships that would otherwise be *absurd* to even contemplate.

God cracks me up.

I find myself shaking my head and laughing when I consider the unusual array of people Dale and I call our friends. They run the gamut from college professors to high school dropouts, from law enforcement officers to ex-convicts—and in many cases the only common thread is God, who in a variety of ways brought us to the same place.

Hollywood has been really nasty to church people, usually portraying them as venal, or ignorant, or dangerous, or all three combined. While there are certainly some kooks and scary people who have wrapped themselves in religion, there are kooks and scary people in all areas of society. But they certainly do not make up the mainstream.

In our life, Dale and I have found people of faith to be an incredibly vital part of our lives. They are who we turn to when the load of life gets heavy. And they are the people who, in turn, come to us when something blows up in their lives.

I have a lifelong friend named Tim who knows me about as well as anyone on the planet, who has seen the good, the bad, and the ugly, and with whom I would literally trust my life. Similarly, Tim would trust me with, well, if not his life, at least his *car* (the older one, and only as long as I show him my insurance card and promise to be back before dark).

But there are *other* guys with whom he would trust his life, so the point is that you can find these kinds of deep and rich relationships as long as you look in the right place.

Dale has her own circle of friends as well, with roots that go back many years.

"I think most women need at least three good friends to make it in life," says Dale. "But being married to you, I need to increase that by a factor of ten."

Har-dee-har.

I occasionally ship Dale off to a friend's house for a day trip or a weekend when she starts to mutter things like, "You are so MALE!" or when I notice she is getting that glazed "prairie woman" look.

Vital Marriage Point: Even though your marriage is your primary and most important relationship, it is *not* self-sustaining like one of those completely sealed little "eco globes" with guppies that you see in the stores. In fact, if your spouse starts to sort of look like one of those little guppies, you REALLY need a break from each other.

Your marriage *needs* outside input to really thrive.

Scan a Bible sometime and note all the times that the phrase "one another" pops up. We are to "love one another" and "serve one another" and "confess our sins to one another" and "pray for one another" and "consider one another as more important than ourselves." Sometimes these statements are in the context of marriage, but more often than not they are in the broader context of the community of faith.

These are not merely good suggestions, they are commands. God is telling us to enter into the kinds of relationships in which we could actually confess our sins to a friend and they would be willing to pray for us and help us instead of rat on us or recoil from us.

Your marriage is not designed to carry the entire load. You need some good friends, both mutual friends and individual friends.

I find that women tend to be pretty open to building deep friendships with other women, but guys are somewhat more reluctant to really open up. In fact, generally speaking, a guy could be involved in a horrific crash on the freeway and be trapped in crumpled metal with his pancreas relocated to his elbow, and if another guy ran up to the car to help, the victim would reply, "I'm fine. Really. Just a scratch. I'll just pound out the dents and be on my way as soon as I get the manifold out of my ear."

Since God knows we are quite willing to act like shallow, pathetic dolts, He does not give us the *option* of having serious, honest relationships, He *orders* us to do it, and part of that directive includes being involved with a church.

Joining a church family and getting *truly* involved in the lives of other people may seem uncomfortable and awkward at first, and it may seem like you have NOTHING in common with these people. You may say to yourself, "Frankly, I really don't think I'm into this."

To which God replies, "Too bad. Do it anyway."*

---

*This is a paraphrase, but the sentiment is definitely there.

Dale and I are good friends with several couples who are still married today because of the caring, concerned advice and friendship of another Christian couple.

This is God's way. He is standing by, ready to help in your time of need, but often cleverly camouflaged beneath the skin of a friend.

Sometimes that skin has scary tattoos, the last vestiges of a former life. But don't be fooled by that. Look up, and you'll see Him in the eyes that dance with light, understanding, and love.

CHAPTER 29

On Not Failing to Avoid Communicating Unclearly With the Selfsame Individual With Whom You, Hereinafter Referred to as "The Party of the First Part," Filed an Amended Tax Return (as it were)

Dale grabbed the ringing phone, listened for a moment, and replied, "You're delivering *what?* Are you sure? Just a moment, please."

She then looked at me with absolute bewilderment, her brow deeply etched.

"Why am I being asked if we are ready to have a refrigerator delivered?" she whispered with her hand cupped over the mouthpiece.

"Well, they probably wanted to make sure we were home," I replied. "Tell them it's fine."

"What are you TALKING about? What refrigerator?!!"

"The new one, obviously," I replied. "They certainly wouldn't be delivering the old one."

I had to take over the phone lest Dale sound completely irrational.

"They'll be here in thirty minutes," I said after I'd hung up. "Boy did you sound grumpy on the phone. Did someone wake up on the wrong side of the bed?"

Dale took a very deep breath.

"Dave, I am going to try to be very calm. Let's take it from the top. This is the first I have heard about a new refrigerator."

"Dale, we talked about this last week!" I protested.

"I have NO IDEA what you are talking about!!!" she exclaimed, throwing her hands in the air.

This was yet another disturbing example of Dale's poor listening skills.

"Dale, don't you remember when I asked if you thought the rosebushes next to the side gate were too bushy to get something big by them?"

"Y-e-s," she replied cautiously. "I was going to ask why you wanted to know, when you ran out the door to go to work and we never finished the conversation."

"Ohhhh. That's right. I *was* running late. I remember now. But, still, refrigerators are *big*. So you really should have put two and two together."

She made a sound remarkably akin to a deep-sea pearl diver coming up for air before she replied.

"So I was supposed to translate a question about *overgrown rosebushes* into a statement that we are having a *refrigerator* delivered this morning? Not only is that *sheer lunacy*, but did you happen to notice that I just got out of the shower, my hair is all wet, our current refrigerator is full of food, and we are supposed to drive eighty miles to meet Scott and Becky—who we have not seen for an entire year—in just a few hours?"

I grimaced.

"Hon, it sounds like you bit off more than you can chew," I said. "If today was a bad day for a delivery, it would have been helpful if you would have said something earlier. I think you need to work on your communication skills. I mean, I'm not a mind reader."

She took a series of deep breaths. Personally, I thought this was an odd time to begin practicing her pregnancy breathing techniques, as she had not been expecting for fifteen years. But I decided that could wait for another conversation, as she was starting to give me "the look."

Unfortunately, the refrigerator episode is not the first time Dale's communication weaknesses have been on parade. There was also the incident wherein I added flour to the shopping list and she failed to ask any of the logical follow-up questions that would have revealed that I signed her up to make cupcakes for Brad's second-grade class. Fortunately, Brad reminded her the next morning on the way to school. Although she managed to complete the task on time, the fact remains that she could have avoided zipping around the kitchen like a hyperactive poodle if she had simply asked me about it earlier.

Compounding the problem, Dale is very resistant to accepting responsibility for her consistent communication lapses. I keep telling her that this little flaw is nothing to be ashamed of, and that it merely requires more personal discipline to overcome. But this is one of her little "blind spots," ranking right up there with her tendency to forget to ask me if there are any checks I have not yet recorded before she tries to use the ATM card at the store. You'd think she would learn after a while.

It's a good thing that at least one of us is a good communicator, or our life would be in complete disarray.

Because I am an extremely effective communicator, I have the added advantage of being able to economize on words but still fully cover the topic under discussion. Dale has yet to master this technique, as seen in the following example.

DALE: "Honey, sometimes I feel like, well, I'm drifting in life. I wonder what my role is. I mean, sure, I love you and I love our family, and I believe that God wants me to primarily focus my energy on you and the kids, but I wonder if I am unconsciously avoiding something big? It isn't that I am *unhappy*; it's more like *unsure*. I mean, this is my one shot at life. Am I missing some kind of calling, some kind of bigger picture? Am I actually fulfilling the niche that God has in mind for me, or am I only doing a small part of it? But then on the other hand, I start to wonder if I am just feeling insecure because you are always doing these big projects and meeting with all these important people, while most of my life is spent in a support role. Not that a support role isn't important. And I really do get a lot of satisfaction out of helping you and the kids succeed and grow. But can you see what I mean? Does my life really have value in the big scheme of things? Am I making any real, lasting difference in any significant way? Can you understand how I feel?"

ME: "Sure!"

Lesser communicators would feel compelled to carry on at great length, groping for words and restating in a hundred different ways that, yes, they really understand. They could use up an *entire evening* dealing with this subject. But notice how in that single, efficient monosyllable of "Sure!" I managed to compact a truckload of empathy and compassion and understanding into a single manageable communication unit no larger than a standard vitamin.

Regrettably, most women (Dale included) have not mastered this powerful communication skill, nor do they show any likelihood whatsoever of doing so. This appears to be a genetic flaw in their gender.

While guys know exactly what they mean when they say "Sure!" wives literally have no clue. So, in deference to their weakness in this area, it falls to the guy to stoop down to her inefficient, time-consuming, lower communication ability and fully translate "Sure!" so that women can grasp it.

In the aforementioned case, the translation went like this:

ME: "Dale, I think you have it a *lot* harder than I do. And I think I understand why you are feeling a little unsettled and insecure. I have a more well-defined role out in the world, and my job puts me in the limelight sometimes. But honey, I couldn't make it without you. I would be so lost. You are the calm at the center of the storm, and I rely on you more than you can possibly know. It isn't just all the support stuff you do, taking care of our home and doing all the basic stuff that makes it possible for us to have a comfortable life; it is *who you are* for me. I believe with all my heart and soul that you are a blessing from God. And what you do for the kids and me is really, really, really important, even though you may not always be able to see it, and even if we forget sometimes to tell you. Everyone sees the astronauts on TV, but we forget that there are hundreds and hundreds of people working behind the scenes or they would *never* get off the ground. So you are Houston Control, and I know it, even if the world doesn't. Thanks for being there. I love you."

Vital Marriage Point: It may not be efficient, but at least they understand it. And, unlike large appliance deliveries, they'll gladly take it even if it is unexpected.

Scary Official Legal Notice

You know how when you watch a movie video there is always an ominous legal notice saying that if you even THINK about making a copy of the tape you will be wrestled to the ground by an entire squad of heavily armed federal agents who will then give you noogies? Well, this book is likewise protected, the main difference being that if you shove this book into your VCR, you will only see a blank screen, but it will still be more interesting than ANYTHING starring Kevin Costner.

But while very few people would consider copying a book (mostly because the copies would cost more than simply buying another book), many of you WILL make the grave mistake of considering loaning this book to a friend. Well, you'd better think twice.

Not that Dave means to "pull rank" or anything, but he does remind you that he works for the United States Congress and, purely by coincidence, tucked away in a recently enacted Copyright Protection Act, appears the "Dave Meurer Monetary Enhancement Clause." It reads as follows:

``Be it hereby recognized by the House of Representatives assembled—except for Rep. Merkowitz, who was in the rest room at the time—that Dave Meurer still has a huge VISA bill arising from when his complete lemon of a station wagon, hereinafter referred to as 'his complete lemon of a station wagon,' went through not one but *three* transmissions. It is the sense of the Congress, therefore, that readers of Dave's books can *recommend* them to a friend but not *loan* them, as this would result in reduced profits to Dave. Violation of this act will result in very spooky penalties that you don't even want to contemplate.''

Somehow that clause got inserted in the bill very late at night when no one was looking, and while it is profoundly unfair, it is nevertheless the law of the land. Bummer for you.

However, you will be pleased to note that it *is* perfectly legal for you to *buy* your friend a book, or even send *additional* money to Dave via Bethany House Publishers at 11400 Hampshire Avenue South, Minneapolis, MN 55438. Yes, you grateful readers, if you are overcome with emotion because Dave has saved your marriage, you can mail him checks, or ship him crates of cash, or even include him in your will! Is this a great country or what?

However, for those of you who are still toying with the idea of violating the "Dave Meurer Monetary Enhancement Clause," we merely remind you that Congress writes the budget for the Department of Defense, so the U.S. Air Force really kind of owes us one. In fact, we even have a new generation of "smart-aleck" weapons that look like the Three Stooges, and give not only noogies but also wedgies.

Talk about "pulling rank"!

If you have to ask, you don't want to know. Just obey the law and nobody gets hurt.